How I Invest
My Money

Also by Joshua Brown
Backstage Wall Street
Clash of the Financial Pundits

Also by Brian Portnoy
The Investor's Paradox
The Geometry of Wealth

How I Invest My Money

*Finance experts reveal how
they save, spend, and invest*

Edited by
Joshua Brown
and Brian Portnoy

and illustrated by
Carl Richards

Hh

HARRIMAN HOUSE LTD
3 Viceroy Court
Bedford Road
Petersfield
Hampshire
GU32 3LJ
GREAT BRITAIN
Tel: +44 (0)1730 233870

Email: enquiries@harriman-house.com
Website: harriman.house

First published in 2020.
Copyright © Joshua Brown and Brian Portnoy

Paperback ISBN: 978-0-85719-808-2
eBook ISBN: 978-0-85719-809-9

British Library Cataloguing in Publication Data
A CIP catalogue record for this book can be obtained from the British Library.

Illustrated by Carl Richards. Illustrations copyright © Carl Richards.

Cover design by Christopher Parker.

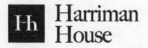

Contents

Introduction

I RAN THE numbers. I've been appearing on financial television for nine and a half years. During those approximately 114 months, I've done an average of three shows each week, which works out to something like 1,368 hours of television time talking about the stock market, the bond market, the economy and investing.

And in all of that time, not one person has ever asked me about what I do with my own money. Not one.

I've commented on everything under the sun: Interest rates, valuation multiples, earnings calls, Federal Reserve policies, tax code changes, housing prices, credit spreads, innovation and technology, consumer confidence, trading strategies, small business ownership, macroeconomics, microeconomics, emerging markets, index funds, active management, shareholder activism, real estate investment trusts, volatility, private equity, venture capital, initial public offerings, oil and gas prices, technical analysis, value investing, momentum stocks, smart beta factors, socially responsible investing, social media, biotechnology and drug approvals, presidential elections, geopolitics, natural disasters, defense contractors, gold and silver, cryptocurrency, high frequency trading, Occupy Wall Street, insider trading, analyst upgrades and downgrades, sectors and industries, long-term investing, day trading, hedge funds, mutual funds, exchange traded funds, gaming companies, sports business, show business, startups, bankruptcies, mergers and acquisitions, and I even interviewed 50 Cent.

And in all of that time, not once did someone say, "Tell us about how you invest *your* money."

It never happened.

It's not that I didn't enjoy commenting on all of these topics, because I did. But looking back on all that time, and all those words coming out of my mouth, I'm amazed that the investing I do with my own money never actually came up!

To remedy this, I wrote a post entitled "How I Invest My Own Money" at The Reformed Broker blog. It was the first time I had ever written at length about how I personally invest, and why I invest the way that I do. The post went viral across all of the social networks I shared it to.

Soon after, I got to talking with my co-author and friend Brian Portnoy about the topic and together we came to the realization that we had the makings of something truly exciting on our hands.

We got to thinking about the fact that very few financial professionals have ever written about their *own* personal finances and investments. We wondered: What if we asked some of our friends and colleagues from around the investing industry about what they do with their own money—and why? No one's ever really done it before.

Between Brian and I, we've read (and written about) hundreds of books on investing. To the best of our recollection, every one of those books was either advice for what *other* people should do, or a focus on a particular investment strategy that the author carries out professionally. Even the hallowed *Market Wizards* series, which we both love, was mostly about how those wizards invested *other people's money*.

Indeed, there is no shortage of books on how experts think *you* ought to invest, but very few of the authors go into detail about whether or not they even take their own advice.

In the pages that follow, you will be reading about investing and money management from a very different perspective. You'll be hearing from some of the most thoughtful and interesting professional investors we know about how they manage their own portfolios.

And more important than the "how" is the "why." During the course of my career, first as a retail broker and then as the CEO of a billion-dollar wealth management firm, I have spoken with thousands of investors, both retail and professional. In that time, I have learned that the reasons why people invest are every bit as important as the names and descriptions of the investments themselves. All of the people in this volume are well-versed in academic investing theories: modern portfolio theory, efficient markets theory, and so forth. But as you'll see, everyone is coming from somewhere unique. Everyone has a story to tell and how we invest, save, and spend is one revealing way of telling that story.

A few years back, I had lunch with a wholesaler for one of the largest asset managers in the world and we got to talking about some of his other clients. The firm he worked for is widely known as a large provider of inexpensive index funds. Without naming names, he told me "If you only knew how many hedge fund managers keep all of their personal capital in index funds with us that cost only a few basis points, you'd be amazed."

I countered that I probably would not be surprised at all. Elaborately allocated and expertly traded portfolios are the quickest route to being able to charge enormous fees. But are they the best solution for those seeking reliable growth and some degree of long-term certainty for their financial futures? Probably not. It made perfect sense to me that people who were already extraordinarily wealthy would want to preserve their wealth using a method very far away from the strategies they use in their professional lives.

As Brian and I set out to populate this book, we made a list of people in the investment industry who we admire both personally and professionally. We wanted to hear about the personal portfolios of people from all different corners of the business—from venture capital, to financial planning, to asset management, and everything in between. We also wanted to bring our idea to potential contributors whom we knew would be honest, open and willing to share the stories of their lives and careers.

I came to a major realization during the course of this project about money, life, and making plans for the future. I've learned that the reasons behind our individual portfolios and investment choices reveal a lot more about us than we might initially think.

Are we too busy helping others to maintain an orderly asset allocation for ourselves?

Are we spending too much time obsessing over formulas, tradeoffs and proportions, to the detriment of remaining focused on the big picture?

Are our personal portfolios an accurate representation of the investment philosophies we espouse in public, or have they deviated from the dogma for one reason or another?

Are we taking more or less risk with our own money than we otherwise would for others? Are we taking redundant risks given the nature of our work?

Do our holdings contain the remnants of poor judgment from the past? Are we overdue for a little maintenance ourselves?

Are we on the same page as the rest of our families; do we have the same aspirations and objectives for the money when the time comes? Can we even agree on the timing?

Have we learned enough along the way to contradict some of our original ideas about how to invest? Are we growing, or closing our minds off to new ideas?

Are we on autopilot or still asking these difficult questions of ourselves?

I'm very excited to share the perspectives and personal stories we've collected for this book from some of the best writers and communicators in the investment business. Brian and I have structured and ordered these chapters in a deliberate way, but we expect many readers to consume them à la carte.

You may find yourself returning to specific chapters more than once, because you came upon a story or strategy that resonated with you. This would make us feel as though the book has achieved its objective.

Nothing would make us happier than to hear that readers were able to learn from the examples of our colleagues and feel more confident in how they're managing their own money.

Picking up this book was a great decision. Please enjoy!

Joshua Brown,
Merrick, New York, 2020

Morgan Housel

Morgan Housel is a partner at the Collaborative Fund and a former columnist at The Motley Fool and *The Wall Street Journal*. He is a two-time winner of the Best in Business Award from the Society of American Business Editors and Writers, winner of the *New York Times* Sidney Award, and a two-time finalist for the Gerald Loeb Award for Distinguished Business and Financial Journalism. His work was featured in *The Best Business Writing* published by the *Columbia Journalism Review*. He is the author of *The Psychology of Money*.

S ANDY GOTTESMAN, A billionaire investor who founded the consulting group First Manhattan, is said to ask one question when interviewing candidates for his investment team: "What do you own, and why?"

Not, "What stocks do you think are cheap?" or "What economy is about to have a recession?"

Just show me what you do with your own money.

I love this question because it highlights what can often be a mile-wide gap between what makes sense—which is what people suggest you do—and what feels right to them—which is what they actually do.

Half of all US mutual fund portfolio managers do not invest a cent of their own money in their funds, according to Morningstar.* This might seem atrocious, and surely the statistic uncovers some hypocrisy.

But this kind of stuff is more common than you'd think. Ken Murray, a professor of medicine at USC, wrote an essay in 2011 titled "How Doctors Die" that showed the degree to which doctors choose different end-of-life treatments for themselves than they recommend for their patients.**

"[Doctors] don't die like the rest of us," he wrote. "What's unusual about them is not how much treatment they get compared to most

---

* A. Ram, *Financial Times*, September 18, 2016.
** K. Murray, Zócalo Public Square, November 30, 2011.

Americans, but how little. For all the time they spend fending off the deaths of others, they tend to be fairly serene when faced with death themselves. They know exactly what is going to happen, they know the choices, and they generally have access to any sort of medical care they could want. But they go gently." A doctor may throw the kitchen sink at her patient's cancer, but choose palliative care for herself.

The difference between what someone suggests you do and what they do for themselves isn't always a bad thing. It just underscores that when dealing with complicated and emotional issues that affect you and your family, there is no one right answer. There is no universal truth.

There's only what works for you and your family, checking the boxes you want checked in a way that leaves you comfortable and sleeping well at night.

There are basic principles that must be adhered to—this is true in finance and in medicine—but important financial decisions are not made in spreadsheets or in textbooks. They are made at the dinner table. They often aren't made with the intention of maximizing returns, but minimizing the chance of disappointing a spouse or child. Those kinds of things are difficult to summarize in charts or formulas, and they vary widely from person to person. What works for one person may not work for another.

You have to find what works for you. Here's what works for me.

How my family thinks about savings

Charlie Munger once said "I did not intend to get rich. I just wanted to get independent."

We can leave aside rich, but independence has always been my personal financial goal. Chasing the highest returns or leveraging my assets to live the most luxurious life has little interest to me. Both look like games people do to impress their friends, and both have hidden risks. I mostly just want to wake up every day knowing my family and

I can do whatever we want to do on our own terms. Every financial decision we make revolves around that goal.

My parents lived their adult years in two stages: dirt poor and moderately well off. My father became a doctor when he was 40 and had three kids. Earning a doctor's salary did not offset the frugal mentality that is forced when supporting three hungry kids while in medical school, and my parents spent the good years living well below their means with a high savings rate.

This gave them a degree of independence. My father was an Emergency Room doctor, one of the highest-stress professions I can imagine and one that requires a painful toggling of circadian rhythms between night and day shifts. After two decades he decided he'd had enough, so he stopped. Just quit. Moved onto the next phase of his life.

That stuck with me. Being able to wake up one morning and change what you're doing, on your own terms, whenever you're ready, seems like the grandmother of all financial goals. Independence, to me, doesn't mean you'll stop working. It means you only do the work you like with people you like at the times you want for as long as you want.

And achieving some level of independence does not rely on earning a doctor's income. It's mostly a matter of keeping your expectations in check and living below your means. Independence, at any income level, is driven by your savings rate. And past a certain level of income your savings rate is driven by your ability to keep your lifestyle expectations from running away.

My wife and I met in college and moved in with each other years before we got married. After school we both had entry-level jobs with entry-level pay, and settled into a moderate lifestyle. All lifestyles exist on a spectrum, and what is decent to one person can feel like royalty or poverty to another. What matters is the savings rate, and at our incomes we got what we considered a decent apartment, a decent car, decent clothes, decent food. Comfortable, but nothing fancy.

Despite more than a decade of rising incomes—myself in finance, my wife in healthcare—we've more or less stayed at that lifestyle ever since. That's pushed our savings rate continuously higher. Virtually every dollar of raise has accrued to savings—our "independence fund." We now live considerably below our means, which tells you little about our income and more about our decision to maintain a lifestyle that we established in our 20s.

If there's a part of our household financial plan I'm proud of it's that we got the goalpost of lifestyle desires to stop moving at a young age. Our savings rate is fairly high, but we rarely feel like we're repressively frugal because our aspirations for more stuff haven't moved much. It's not that our aspirations are nonexistent—we like nice stuff and live comfortably. We just got the goalpost to stop moving.

This would not work for everyone, and it only works for us because we both agree to it equally—neither of us are compromising for the other. Most of what we get pleasure from—going for walks, reading, podcasts—costs little, so we rarely feel like we're missing out. On the rare occasion when I question our savings rate I think of the independence my parents earned from years of high savings, and I quickly come back. Independence is our top goal. A secondary benefit of maintaining a lifestyle below what you can afford is avoiding the psychological treadmill of keeping up with the Joneses. Comfortably living below what you can afford, without much desire for more, removes a tremendous amount of social pressure that many people in the modern first world subject themselves to. Nassim Taleb explained: "True success is exiting some rat race to modulate one's activities for peace of mind." I like that.

We're so far committed to the independence camp that we've done things that make little sense on paper. We own our house without a mortgage, which is the worst financial decision we've ever made but the best money decision we've ever made. Mortgage interest rates were absurdly low when we bought our house. Any rational advisor would recommend taking advantage of cheap money and investing extra savings in higher-return assets, like stocks. But our goal isn't to be coldly rational; just psychologically reasonable.

The independent feeling I get from owning our house outright far exceeds the known financial gain I'd get from leveraging our assets with a cheap mortgage. Eliminating the monthly payment feels better than maximizing the long-term value of our assets. It makes me feel independent.

I don't try to defend this decision to those pointing out its flaws, or those who would never do the same. On paper it's defenseless. But it works for us. We like it. That's what matters. Good decisions aren't always rational. At some point you have to choose between being happy or being "right."

We also keep a higher percentage of our assets in cash than most financial advisors would recommend—something around 20% of our assets outside the value of our house. This is also close to indefensible on paper, and I'm not recommending it to others. It's just what works for us.

We do it because cash is the oxygen of independence, and—more importantly—we never want to be forced to sell the stocks we own. We want the probability of facing a huge expense and needing to liquidate stocks to cover it to be as close to zero as possible. Perhaps we just have a lower risk tolerance than others.

But everything I've learned about personal finance tells me that everyone—without exception—will eventually face a huge expense they did not expect—and they don't plan for these expenses specifically because they did not expect them. The few people who know the details of our finances ask, "What are you saving for? A house? A boat? A new car?" No, none of those. I'm saving for a world where curveballs are more common than we expect. Not being forced to sell stocks to cover an expense also means we're increasing the odds of letting the stocks we own compound for the longest period of time. Charlie Munger put it well: "The first rule of compounding is to never interrupt it unnecessarily."

How my family thinks about investing

I started my career as a stock picker. At the time we only owned individual stocks, mostly large companies like Berkshire Hathaway and Procter & Gamble, mixed with smaller stocks I considered deep value investments. Go back to my 20s and at any given point I held something like 25 individual stocks.

I don't know how I did as a stock picker. Did I beat the market? I'm not sure. Like most who try, I didn't keep a good score. Either way, I've shifted my views and now every stock we own is a low-cost index fund.

I don't have anything against actively picking stocks, either on your own or through giving your money to an active fund manager. I think some people can outperform the market averages—it's just very hard, and harder than most people think.

If I had to summarize my views on investing, it's this: Every investor should pick a strategy that has the highest odds of successfully meeting their goals. And I think for most investors, dollar-cost averaging into a low-cost index fund will provide the highest odds of long-term success.

That doesn't mean index investing will always work. It doesn't mean it's for everyone. And it doesn't mean active stock picking is doomed to fail. In general, this industry has become too entrenched on one side or the other—particularly those vehemently against active investing.

Beating the market should be hard; the odds of success should be low. If they weren't, everyone would do it, and if everyone did it there would be no opportunity. So no one should be surprised that the majority of those trying to beat the market fail to do so. (The statistics show 85% of large-cap active managers didn't beat the S&P 500 over the decade ending 2019.*)

---

* B. Pisani, CNBC, March 15, 2019.

I know people who think it's insane to try to beat the market but encourage their kids to reach for the stars and try to become professional athletes. To each their own. Life is about playing the odds, and we all think about odds a little differently.

Over the years I came around to the view that we'll have a high chance of meeting all of our family's financial goals if we consistently invest money into a low-cost index fund for decades on end, leaving the money alone to compound. A lot of this view comes from our lifestyle of frugal spending. If you can meet all your goals without having to take the added risk that comes from trying to outperform the market, then what's the point of even trying? I can afford to not be the greatest investor in the world, but I can't afford to be a bad one. When I think of it that way, the choice to buy the index and hold on is a no-brainer for us. I know not everyone will agree with that logic, especially my friends whose job it is to beat the market. I respect what they do. But this is what works for us.

We invest money from every paycheck into these index funds—a combination of US and international stocks. There's no set goal— it's just whatever is left over after we spend. We max out retirement accounts in the same funds, and contribute to our kids' 529 college savings plans.

And that's about it. Effectively all of our net worth is a house, a checking account, and some Vanguard index funds.

It doesn't need to be more complicated than that for us. I like it simple. One of my deeply held investing beliefs is that there is little correlation between investment effort and investment results. The reason is because the world is driven by tails—a few variables account for the majority of returns. No matter how hard you try at investing you won't do well if you miss the two or three things that move the needle in your strategy. The reverse is true. Simple investment strategies can work great as long as they capture the few things that are important to that strategy's success. My investing strategy doesn't rely on picking the right sector, or timing the next recession. It relies on a high savings rate, patience, and optimism that the global economy will create value over the next several decades. I spend virtually all of my investing effort thinking about those three things—especially the first two, which I can control.

I've changed my investment strategy in the past. So of course there's a chance I'll change it in the future.

No matter how we save or invest I'm sure we'll always have the goal of independence, and we'll always do whatever maximizes for sleeping well at night.

We think it's the ultimate goal; the mastery of the psychology of money.

But to each their own. No one is crazy.

Christine Benz

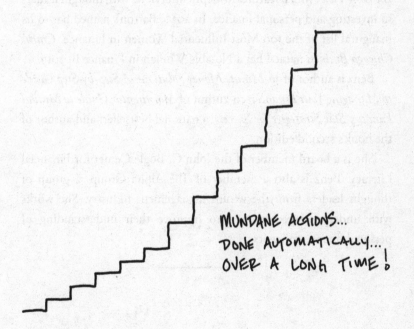

MUNDANE ACTIONS...
DONE AUTOMATICALLY...
OVER A LONG TIME!

Christine Benz

———————

Christine Benz is Director of Personal Finance for Morningstar and senior columnist for Morningstar.com. She also co-hosts a podcast, *The Long View*, which features in-depth interviews with thought leaders in investing and personal finance. In 2020, Barron's named her to its inaugural list of the 100 Most Influential Women in Finance. *Crain's Chicago Business* named her a Notable Woman in Finance in 2019.

Benz is author of *30-Minute Money Solutions: A Step-by-Step Guide to Managing Your Finances*; co-author of *Morningstar Guide to Mutual Funds: 5-Star Strategies for Success*, a national bestseller; and author of the book's second edition.

She is a board member of the John C. Bogle Center for Financial Literacy. Benz is also a member of The Alpha Group, a group of thought leaders from the wealth management industry. She works with underprivileged women to improve their understanding of personal finance concepts.

———————

I'LL NEVER BE passionate about investments.

That's not a comfortable admission, given that I've spent my career in a job where investments are central, and I work amid people who are deeply, truly, genuinely *into* investments. I have colleagues who get very excited about researching the performance difference between two bond ETFs, and others who like nothing better than listening to mutual fund managers noodle over their stock picks.

That's not me. But I've made peace with it, because I've realized that what I am passionate about is investors, and most of them aren't passionate about investments, either. Rather, they view investments as a means to an end—a way to help pay for college for their kids or to find financial security in retirement. For them, getting the big stuff right—living within their means, setting a reasonable savings rate, staying employed—will be a bigger determinant of whether they reach their goals than will their investment selections. A streamlined, low-cost, and utilitarian portfolio is the way to go.

My husband and I try to manage our financial affairs in that same way, so that we can stay focused on what matters most to us: working in careers that we find rewarding; pursuing our shared passions of music, food, and travel; being engaged in our community; and staying close to family. One of my sisters has an intellectual disability and lives with us for a part of each year; seeing to her well-being and happiness is a key priority for us, especially since my mom and dad have passed away over the past decade.

To help keep everything as simple as possible, we maintain just a handful of accounts, and we've been able to do that largely because we've both been employed at the same firms for more than 25 years. (Yes, dinosaurs. I know!) We each have 401(k)s, and then we have our taxable assets and IRAs at Vanguard. I also have a health savings account. We also have checking and savings accounts at an old-money Chicago bank. We joke that we are their worst customers ever; we try not to keep much money in those accounts, just what we need to fund cash flows, and we don't use any services, unless you count getting foreign currency before trips and using their online bill-paying and ATMs.

Within my Morningstar 401(k), I have both active and passive funds, but mainly active. My account is primarily equities. I steer a fourth of my contribution into four equity funds: Vanguard Institutional Index, American Funds Washington Mutual (the R6 share class—0.27% expense ratio), Vanguard International Growth, and Dodge & Cox International. I've been contributing to those four funds for the past five years or more. Vanguard International Growth is my largest position; I think I've held that fund since I joined Morningstar in 1993. I have been making Roth 401(k) contributions for the past decade or so, but I still have a healthy share of my balance in the traditional 401(k). Morningstar recently added a provision that allows us to make after-tax contributions and convert them to Roth inside the plan. I plan to start using that feature, because it will allow me to get more money inside the plan, above and beyond the baseline 401(k) contributions that you're allowed to make, and amass more in the Roth column, too. It's a more tax-efficient use of funds than investing in a taxable account.

My husband's 401(k) is mostly all passive, though his bond exposure is PIMCO Total Return. He has a bit more in bonds in his 401(k) than I do in mine, but not much.

We hold our taxable assets at Vanguard; we have money that goes in on autopilot every month. We just have a few funds: Vanguard

Primecap Core, Developed Markets Index, Intermediate-Term Tax-Exempt, and Tax-Exempt Money Market. We make monthly contributions to all, but larger amounts to the equity funds. I am sure the whole thing could be a touch more tax-efficient, especially if we used a total market index fund or ETF for our US equity exposure. But we have owned Primecap Core in that account since it opened, so switching out of that one, in particular, would trigger capital gains. I try not to worry too much about issues like this; the small stuff matters, of course, but getting the big stuff right is what makes or breaks a plan. We have more safe investments in this account than we do elsewhere, largely because it has always felt right to have our more liquid assets where we could actually access them if we need them.

We started doing the backdoor Roth IRA when that maneuver became available in 2010; we each fund traditional IRAs annually, then convert to Roth. When we started with this program, we used Morningstar's X-Ray feature to examine our portfolio's positioning. At the time we noticed that we were light on foreign stocks and value, so we added Vanguard International Value. It's the sole holding in both of our IRAs. We're subject to the limits on IRAs for new contributions so the accounts aren't big, but they've grown nicely since we started funding them, and it'll be nice to have a source of funds in retirement that isn't taxed or subject to RMDs.

I've also been funding my health savings account to the maximum allowable amount since Morningstar added the high-deductible healthcare plan as an option a few years ago. It's not a huge account at this point, but we try to pay any health-care expenses with non-HSA assets so the account can grow. It's amazing how powerful those ongoing contributions can be, and how painless they are when they come directly out of my paycheck.

To the extent that this has all worked, I think that owes to a few factors, all incredibly mundane. The first and biggest is just that we've both been consistently employed throughout our careers, and that has allowed us to save consistently, too. We have pretty much everything on autopilot for contributions at this point, including our taxable contributions, and have done so for many years.

My husband and I have also been lucky to be on the same page with respect to money matters. He has always been a saver but is never cheap about things that matter, and early on he influenced me to be that same way. The fact that we agree on how we spend our money is, I think, a reflection of the fact that we share similar values. For example, I recently suggested that we provide some financial help to someone in our lives who needed it. I was a little nervous about mentioning it, fearing that he might think it overly generous. But his response was, "Oh, absolutely; we should do that." I think that being financially compatible with your partner is a hugely under-discussed factor in financial success.

Also in the category of luck, I've gotten Morningstar stock for much of my career, and the stock has done well. I've tried to skinny down my positions in a tax-efficient way over the years, but, objectively, holding a concentrated position in my employer's stock adds risk to our plan. I hold some Morningstar Inc. shares outright, and also have restricted stock units. We've met with a fantastic hourly financial planning firm in the Chicago area that has a lot of expertise in company stock, so they've been helpful in strategizing about how to reduce the stake without taking a big tax hit.

Another key factor working in our favor has been that we've been pretty equity-heavy all along. We both know that markets move in cycles, so we've never gotten bothered during the normal downturns that happen. In fact, I often have to feign that I understand that people get spooked and rattled during market volatility. But if I am honest, I am just not in touch with those feelings at all. I wouldn't rule out that the next market downturn will affect me more meaningfully, though, because the last one was 10 years ago, and now we're 10 years older and that much closer to retirement.

We own a house that we love, but we don't consider it an investment. When we were younger we may have, especially because we put a lot of sweat equity into our first house and it was fun to watch our equity grow. That equity was a pretty big percentage of our net worth back then. At this life stage, though, our home is the place where we live, not an investment. If we were to move, it's likely that we would spend a like amount of money on housing, so housing-related assets just don't really figure into my thinking when I think about our assets.

If we have made mistakes, the main issue would be that we always have quite a bit of cash knocking around in our taxable account mainly because of inertia and because it never feels like a great time to move it all into something with more return potential. There has surely been an opportunity cost in that, especially as cash yields have gone close to zero at various points in time in recent years. On the other hand, knowing that we have liquid reserves that we could tap in a pinch probably gives us peace of mind to stay very aggressive with our retirement accounts.

I'm a firm believer that success in life is all about finding balance, and I think my investments reflect that.

Brian Portnoy

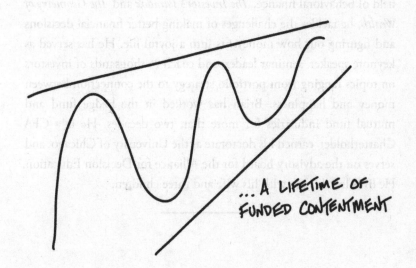

... A LIFETIME OF
FUNDED CONTENTMENT

Brian Portnoy is the founder of Shaping Wealth, a financial wellness platform that engages with individuals and organizations to make better money decisions. In his two highly acclaimed books in the field of behavioral finance, *The Investor's Paradox* and *The Geometry of Wealth*, he tackles the challenges of making better financial decisions and figuring out how money fits into a joyful life. He has served as keynote speaker, seminar leader, and coach to thousands of investors on topics ranging from portfolio strategy to the connection between money and happiness. Brian has worked in the hedge fund and mutual fund industries for more than two decades. He is a CFA Charterholder, earned his doctorate at the University of Chicago, and serves on the advisory board for the Alliance for Decision Education. He lives in Chicago with his wife and three children.

M Y PARENTS FOUGHT about money all the time. It's not that we were lacking. My dad made good money and my mom was good at spending it. They didn't seem to like each other for many reasons, and money served as both a language of conflict and a currency of control. Following the divorce, issues of alimony and child support extended the unpleasantries for decades.

Fast forward to recent times, I'm sometimes asked what I learned from my parents about money. The short answer is always: Nothing. A longer, harsher answer is that money is a tool: to buy things and to hurt others.

It would be easy to connect the dots and conclude that my current career focused around financial wellness somehow addresses the pain of a difficult childhood. Sounds good, but it's not true. My 20-year career in money world started accidentally. In 2000, I left academia and joined Morningstar. I was broke, I wanted to marry Tracy (now my wife of 20 years), I didn't want to schlep from one professorship to the next, and Morningstar hired other oddballs like me who could write well and found markets interesting. How I have come to invest is not the answer to a Freudian riddle but an adaptive solution to an evolving life with people I love and ideas I cherish.

My thoughts around money life—not just investing, but earning, spending, saving, borrowing, giving, and so forth—have coalesced around the notion of "funded contentment." True wealth, I believe, is the ability to underwrite a life that is meaningful *to me*. This is very different than being rich, or merely having more. Funded contentment is my mental model for thinking about the life I want to lead, and the lives of my wife and three kids.

I joke (sort of) that I should write a book called "Sandwiched" about life as a parent of growing kids and child of aging parents. Tackling either challenge is a handful. Tackling both is exhausting—and expensive.

We have a few goals. The first is living a day-to-day life of convenience with as little aggravation as possible, such that we can afford a meaningful life—one filled with deep connections, wonderful experiences (especially travel), professional achievement, and some sense that we're living for something beyond ourselves.

Then there are the twin pillars of college and retirement. If Ben, Zach, and Sarah each go to a four-year private university, I'm out about a million bucks. What we need for retirement is a guess (yes, I know all the numbers, calculators, cash flow metrics, but still), so we're maxing out 401(k)s and IRAs.

The third goal is to leave the kids without the financial burden of caring for me and Tracy. Helping to support my mom is unpleasant. So I've sworn to not be a financial burden to my children later in life.

Finally, there is my sister Cheryl. She is developmentally disabled with a genetic condition called Fragile X and will always need my help. It is stressful to know I will need to care for her for the rest of her life, but it also a deep source of contentment that I am on target to have the money to do so. My dad has long supported her, but in due course, it's all on me.

In funding all of this, mental accounting is my friend. I love the line that all models are wrong but some are useful, as it reflects the pragmatism I want to bring to managing my money life. So first, as described above, there are categories of things I need to underwrite, ranging from big lump-sum payments like college to regular cash flows both for life now and in retirement. And then there are the means of doing all that. I have four buckets:

1. Free beta
2. Juicy cash
3. Enterprise income
4. Long-term options

Before I detail those, some comments on lifestyle. In a successful money life, investing is the easiest part—if you can cut through the noise. The crux of money life starts with the other things: first earning, and then spending, saving, and borrowing.

It's not false modesty to say that I've been luckier than good to hover around the perimeter of the hedge fund industry for a long time and make some good money along the way. I have no qualms taking advantage of an amoral ecosystem that I could leverage for my own purposes. In the context of high earnings, Tracy and I have been disciplined in our spending, not because of a rigorous budget, but because we just don't covet the big ticket items (cars, jewelry, wine, art, fancy travel) that seem to seduce others. Thus, the bedrock of our financial health has been our disposition to save and, by the same token, an aversion to debt. We paid off our mortgage a while ago. I know the "spread" on what I might have earned with that cash. I don't care. I love not having a mortgage, and no other debt to speak of.

With earning, spending, saving, and borrowing in check, there is then investing. Let me dive into my four buckets.

Free beta. One could write an entire book on how picking "better" fund managers is a fool's errand (actually I did) and my takeaway after two decades of having a backstage pass to the best fund managers in the world is: Nearly all of us nearly all of the time should own stock and bond beta index funds (or ETFs), allocate to them in reasonable proportions, and then get on with life. Most of our college and retirement assets are in the Vanguard Total World Stock ETF (VT). At 9 basis points per year (almost free), VT delivers globally diversified equity exposure. If the global stock market does well, we'll do well. I have zero interest in actively tilting my portfolio by region or sector or other factors. It's worse than a coin flip's chance I'd get any of that right. I know lots of very rich fund managers who do this for a living and tend to get it wrong. I'd rather read a book.

Juicy cash. On paper, the biggest investing mistake I've made is holding too much cash. At times, it's been north of 25% of our total net worth. The back of the envelope math on what I could have earned on that cash over the decade-long bull market is stomach turning. Still, here's my thinking. First, my career has an extremely high market beta. My human capital and financial capital are closely correlated. Times like 2008 put my financial—and family—stability at risk. I need to hedge that. I have had many finance jobs, left some willingly, others not, and cash hedges my liabilities, both cash flow and emotional. I've long slept well knowing that no matter what, Tracy and the kids would be fine for a long stretch (years) if my career really tanked. More constructively, I've come to see cash as providing optionality to take advantage of market dislocations or unexpected opportunities.

The "juicy" part is my effort to earn higher returns in a zero-to-low rate world. Unlike others, I've not hopscotched to different banks offering marginally higher rates. The hassle doesn't seem worth a few extra basis points. Instead, I've tried to park my cash in short-term municipal bond offerings with outsized yields. I invest in a small private fund (limited partnership) which buys short-duration, odd lot munis with tax-equivalent yields north of 5%. These opportunities are out there if you look for them and big institutional muni buyers can't touch them. One could say that is bond investing, not cash, and that's fine. The fund has monthly (not daily) liquidity, which allows the PMs to manage the fund effectively.

Enterprise income. Tracy and I own a couple real estate properties that generate recurring income. I love the feeling of that rent coming in every month. My dream is to get to a point in my 60s where I have a substantial amount of rock-steady income that more than underwrites our day-to-day when healthy and our needs when not.

In addition to those positions of indefinite duration, we've also invested in shorter-duration private loans. These are a weird hodgepodge of opportunities that stem from having access to networks of private investors. They tend to be some form of convertible, preferred, or senior debt security with an attractive payoff for the risk and, when possible, some upside potential on the back end. For example, I was part of a small syndicate which loaned a quarry owner money to buy new rock crushing equipment. Due to idiosyncratic factors, he didn't have bank financing available to him, so a mutual friend structured a note with a mid-teens percentage return. I also have several senior debt positions in buildings that are leased primarily by government entities. Again, for idiosyncratic reasons, I'm earning high single digits on my loans, plus have some upside in the value of the buildings should they sell in the next few years. In all of this, access is critical. There are good lessons here for how social capital transforms into financial capital.

Long-term options. This is a bucket of uncertain angel and venture capital investments. To date, I've owned or continue to own stakes in a number of tiny companies that I hope will succeed. Some have done just that, including a craft whiskey manufacturer which sold itself to a spirits brand aggregator. Same with a medical cannabis operator. Others are already zeros or are zombies on the cusp of zero (what an awful feeling). Most are alive and kicking. For example, a dear friend started a cool company that provides meditation services to corporate clients. I invested $25,000 because I'm rooting for her. She's killing it but even if it falters, I'll know I supported my friend. Generally, if a few of these hit, I will make "a lot" of money. The actual number is a total guess and to peg my financial plan on one would be foolish. These are lottery tickets.

In conclusion, money can serve both chaos and control. I know from my day jobs that the control part is elusive, and that playing the odds is about the best we can do. There's a lot that can go wrong in what I've discussed and there's no Monte Carlo simulation that can begin to capture what it is, since much of the downside is personal, not statistical. Funding contentment, so it seems, is not a "number" to hit or an age to achieve, but an ongoing quest to afford what really matters.

Joshua Brown

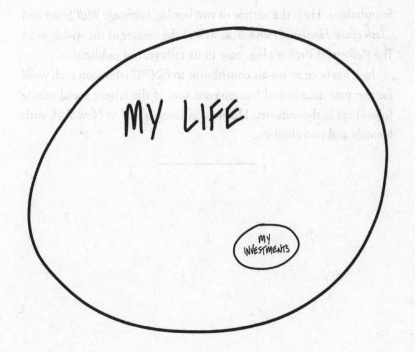

MY LIFE

MY INVESTMENTS

"Downtown" Josh Brown is the co-founder and Chief Executive Officer of Ritholtz Wealth Management, which manages over $1.3 billion for individual investors, corporate retirement plans, endowments and foundations. He is the author of two books, *Backstage Wall Street* and *Clash of the Financial Pundits*, as well as the creator of the widely-read The Reformed Broker blog, now in its 12th year of publication.

Josh has been an on-air contributor to CNBC television each week for the past decade and has amassed one of the largest social media followings in the industry. He lives on Long Island in New York with his wife and two children.

H OW DO I invest my personal money?
Very simply put, I'm a mixture of active and passive, a mixture of mutual funds, individual securities and ETFs, a mixture of public and private assets.

What is consistent is that almost everything I do is with a long-term bias. I don't day trade or swing trade, because I'm bad at it and I feel as though those activities are a full-time commitment. I don't want to commit to any investing style that requires my attention all day long because I'm building and running a company. My priority is my firm, my clients and my employees. So when I invest in something, I usually intend to stay invested.

First things first, the bulk of my net worth is in my house, with no mortgage. We've been spending money on remodeling over the last few years – not for any kind of payoff, but because we intend to live there forever. So this is more of a psychic investment than it is a financial one. I love my home and have no intention of selling. We've renovated and decorated it for ourselves and our own happiness. If I sold today, I might see a profit because people are fleeing New York City and making million-dollar offers to brokers over the phone for homes in my town, but then I'd have to buy something else at an elevated price. For what?

My other big investment is the 30-something percent I own of Ritholtz Wealth Management (RWM). We did a dilution last year in order to facilitate the first wave of equity partners buying in. Our intention is to be employee-owned, and to only make decisions that will benefit our clients and employee-partners going forward. The firm is entirely bootstrapped from day one – no private equity, no debt, no outside investors. This is both strategically and emotionally important to us.

My 401(k) is invested in the exact same asset allocation model as we use for our clients. I own the same funds, in the same proportions, that my clients of comparable risk tolerance own. I'm in an all-equity model because I'm relatively young, can bear risk and will not be accessing this capital for at least another 25 years.

Every other employee of Ritholtz Wealth is also invested in the same asset allocation models as our clients. This was a very important decision we made early on. We eat our own cooking with our own personal retirement accounts. I consider the combination of my 401(k) invested in our client strategies along with my equity stake in the firm to be my "real money." I've made the bet of a lifetime on our advice and our business.

I've got a SEP IRA and some rollovers from previous employers. I utilize the tax-deferred benefits of those accounts to hold individual stocks, along with some of the ETFs my friends have launched over the years. These are funds that aren't part of our client strategies. I believe in supporting my friends when they launch stuff. I don't mind having friends run a portion of my money and I never judge them against the S&P 500. I just don't care about that. I have enough invested in Vanguard or iShares indexes already.

The Wall Street Journal once did a story on the personal investments of Jack Bogle. Bogle's son had managed hedge funds and currently manages active small cap funds, which charge a hell of a lot more than the index funds at Vanguard. Jack, the godfather of passive investing, invested in his son's active funds.

I admired his explanation for these investments:

> But Jack Bogle, a relentless advocate for low fees, does poke fun at his son's prosperity.

"I often tease him," Jack Bogle says. His son's firm manages about $1.1 billion and its small-cap mutual fund charges annual fees of 1.35%, much higher than the 0.24% annual fee for a Vanguard index fund that tracks similar stocks, but about average for active managers offering similar services.

John Bogle has a ready reply: He is making money for clients and for himself. "Is there anything wrong with that?" he said once in response.

This year, John Bogle's fund has generated total returns of 40%... according to Morningstar, compared with 35% for the Russell 2000 and 34% for the similar Vanguard fund, according to Morningstar.

Even his father benefits. He is an investor in the small-cap fund. "We come about it very differently, but we end up pretty close to the same place," the elder Mr. Bogle says. "He's done what he's done very well... Will it work forever? I don't know. But I'm not going to bet against him."

Indeed, the elder Mr. Bogle's stake in his son's mutual fund is one of his few nonindex investments. "We do some things for family reasons," he says. "If it's not consistent, well, life isn't always consistent."

That's right. Life isn't always consistent.

I also own two dozen individual stocks. Mostly companies where I am a fan, user and customer of their products and services. JPMorgan, Slack, Starbucks, Shake Shack, Apple, Amazon, Google, Verizon, Uber, etc. I buy these things and don't sell them. I add to them when opportunities present themselves. I automatically reinvest the dividends. When I'm paying my Verizon wireless bill or my Fios cable bill, I smile knowing that I'm contributing to my own company. It's a mental trick I've developed to keep me from bailing on them in tough markets.

Another advantage of the IRAs is that I'm not taxed on REIT distributions, which would normally hit me as ordinary income. So I've been building a position in STORE Capital, Invitation Homes and Prologis, three of my favorites, using dividend reinvestment. I root for them to go down so that when I get a distribution, I can buy even more shares at a lower price. A friend of mine who is a major real estate developer on Long Island talked me out of buying real estate on my own, or in the private market. He explained how futile it would be for me to do something like that as a hobby, or with smaller dollar amounts than the real players. His arguments were convincing, so I turned to REITs instead of getting clowned in the commercial real estate market by the professionals and developers.

I'm not buying individual stocks because I think I'm going to generate alpha. I just love stocks and have ever since I was 20 years old. And it's my money, I get to do whatever I want with it. *Life isn't always consistent.*

I did my children's 529 plans with the state of New York, which is Vanguard index funds. Their grandparents funded most of what's there when they were born, and we add to it each year. I probably see a statement every three years or so, LOL. I have to look up how to log in and see it, I have no clue. Better off. My oldest won't be going to college for four more years.

Finally, with the taxable money that's left over, we fund the Liftoff account that's meant for the kids when they get older. Liftoff is an automated asset management platform RWM built in partnership with Betterment. There is no minimum and it's a way for us to help younger investors who are in the process of wealth accumulation today.

I have to balance the need to put money away for my kids when they're older with the desire to do things for them now, like family vacations. We can't do everything, so there are many ongoing conversations about the value of experiences today versus having assets tomorrow. My wife and I had my partner and firm co-founder Kris Venne come over and do a financial plan for us a few years ago, which helped us out a lot in making these decisions. So not only do I invest alongside my clients, I get the same financial planning advice as they do too.

Outside of these traditional investments, I am an investor in a small handful of startups that I believe in. I've got shares of Vestwell, Digital Assets Data Corporation and Riskalyze, and serve on the advisory boards of all three companies. We love their software and use it within our practice. I'm proud to be affiliated with founders like Aaron Schumm, Mike Alfred and Aaron Klein, and all that they've built. I have a small stake in the social network StockTwits, which keeps me plugged in to what's going on with the active trader community.

I am frequently offered shares in fintech startups with the expectation that I will use my fame to help put the company on the map. I say "no thank you." I prefer to be involved with companies whose products or services I actually use. There's no such thing as "free" in this world, and being offered stock in a fintech startup is no different. They may not want my money, but they definitely want my time or my influence or something else that I will not part with.

I began casually investing in pre-IPO startups with the EquityZen platform this year. EquityZen puts a new fund together every year and buys stocks in privately-held, venture-backed startups that the firm believes have a bright future. Two recent inclusions to the fund are Unity Technologies and Instacart. It's hard to know which startups will become the technology giants of tomorrow and which will fizzle out, which is why the basket approach of EquityZen makes sense for me. I don't have the time, attention, expertise or capital to make these sorts of investments directly.

One major life lesson I've learned over the years is to never argue the merits of my own portfolio with anyone else. There will always be people who criticize how others invest and what they invest in, but these arguments are usually coming from a place of insecurity and doubt. If you're confident in what you're doing, then the last thing in the world you're worried about is what other people are doing. And when people disagree with you about a stock or a sector bet, there's a very simple way to resolve the conflict—time. If you're so smart and I'm so dumb, then you'll make a lot of money betting against me. Or not. We'll see what happens. Worry about your own portfolio and I'll focus on my own.

You will never see me engaging in public arguments with investors about their holdings because I literally could not care less what other people think. Get yourself to that place mentally as fast as you can. Stock message boards are a toxic waste dump. Those pockets of online discussion where differences over investment styles devolve into personal attacks should be avoided. There are people who use these forums in order to throw rocks to make themselves feel better. No one is forcing you to stand there and participate. I know thousands of professionals in our industry. None of them conduct themselves this way.

My asset allocation and outside bets make sense only for me, just like your portfolio ought to make sense only for you. There is no such thing as a one-size-fits-all portfolio, because we all have different time horizons, risk factors, wants and needs, and emotional triggers. I figured out what works for me, but only after a lot of trial and error over the last two decades. And lots of mistakes.

A skilled advisor is not just someone who knows investments— it's someone who knows their clients well enough to know what combination of investments will work *for each person*. Serving as my own advisor, I've learned to differentiate between what works for other people and what works for me personally.

Bob Seawright

Robert P. Seawright is the Chief Investment Officer for Madison Avenue Securities, LLC, a boutique investment advisory firm and broker-dealer in San Diego, California, where he lives with his wife Ginny, a fifth grade teacher. They have three grown children and eight grandchildren. He has degrees from the State University of New York and Duke University.

DEATH AND HER 89th birthday were fighting for control as Mimi lay on a third-floor hospital bed in a drab North Jersey hospital one cold January day. It didn't matter which won, Mimi was going to lose, and soon, no matter what.

She had lived 20 years without Pop, much of that time in failing health and blindness. Mimi was ready to go.

Her family stood vigil beside her. In a testimony to her life and legacy, Mimi's room was overflowing with each of her four children, ten grandchildren and eight great-grandchildren, including my wife Ginny, our children, and our grandchildren.

Songs were sung, old stories and jokes were retold, and memories were shared, yet again. Muted birthday wishes were offered. Even though (and because) Mimi didn't get all of it, heads were frequently turned away to hide wet, tear-stained faces.

It was time.

I watched Mimi's grandchildren and their bedside manner. I listened to them. I grieved with and for them. The most consistent point to their reminiscences was their gratitude for being able to spend summers at Mimi's cottage in the Adirondack Mountains of New York.

Ginny first visited the Adirondacks in Mimi's womb and has returned summer after summer ever since.

When she and Pop bought the cottage in 1980, Mimi was adamant that it was for the express purpose of spending more time in an area the family loved and providing a place for their children and (then prospective) grandchildren to gather. It became the family retreat.

Our children have spent some or all of every summer of their lives there. They hiked there. They swam there. They played tetherball there. They canoed there. They waterskied there. As teenagers, they got summer jobs there. Our daughter met her husband there.

Perhaps most importantly, there was time at the cottage. Conversations were had, values were imparted (in the best way, without the kids realizing), lessons learned, relationships repaired, memories made. We invested in each other.

The cottage is a remarkable family fulcrum. Its environs were and remain our children's favorite place in the world, and they have passed that love down to their own children. Mimi's legacy is broader and deeper than the cottage, of course, but it is inextricably tied to it.

The cottage was a great investment. It was a mechanism for Mimi to get and keep her family together. It served her purpose.

We in the financial world spend enormous amounts of time considering how we (and our clients) should invest. We ought to spend more time than we usually do considering and reminding ourselves why we invest. We save and invest for the future, obviously, but what we want that future to look like depends upon our "whys"— what we have determined are the purposes by which we choose to live.

I am confident every contributor to this book offers similar investment and financial planning strategies including, in no particular order: simplicity; aggressive saving; a balanced lifestyle; diversification; low costs; a sensible asset allocation consistent with one's goals, risk capacity, and risk tolerance; smart asset location; careful tax/estate planning and management; and a focus on the power of compound interest. I do too, and it's all important.* The whys are more important.

---

* Here are a few specifics about how Ginny and I invest our money. Because Ginny is a teacher, she has a 403(b) and a good pension. I have a 401(k) and we have a joint investment account. We invest in low-cost, globally diversified

One's purposes provide the foundation upon which a financial plan is built. A good financial plan is designed to provide a means and the funding for living out one's life… on purpose.

Humans generally lack courage more than genius, and persistence most of all. Accordingly, sticking with our financial plans is often more difficult than creating and implementing a good one. Repeated consideration and articulation of our purposes can help us do that. Imagining ourselves at the end of life—like Mimi in that hospital bed—thinking back over life's joys, struggles, and decisions, can prod us toward better and more profound choices.

Our decision-making systems default toward immediate, tangible rewards, which means we are prone to short-change or ignore investments in intangible, longer-term initiatives. It's easy to lose sight of our purposes when life happens to us.

Everyone faces hardship. Some hardships and difficulties are random and out of our control, others are earned by poor choices and poor planning. By taking the initiative with good planning, we can provide for better opportunities and seek better outcomes.

There is frequently a gaping hole between the life people say they want and the life they live, and that gap is routinely self-inflicted. If your marriage, your family life, or your relationships generally are

---

funds and use Roth vehicles to the extent we can (partly because we think taxes will be higher later, but mostly because we like the idea of having tax obligations out of the way). We own no individual stocks and no derivatives. We rebalance automatically. We overweight foreign stocks because of the better values available there, but recognize that bet may not pay off. Because we try to live simply and because Ginny's pension and my Social Security will cover our expected living expenses in retirement, we have a much lower exposure to bonds than is typical for people our age. Were those retirement income streams not available to us, we would use an annuity for guaranteed income. Because we are long-term investors, I only look at our statements twice a year, which also provides personal volatility management. If I get the urge to trade, I look at off-the-beaten-path securities that institutions don't care about, in small size, like closed-end funds holding names I like trading at steep discounts to NAV, or odd-lot municipal bonds. We also own securities created by people like Perth Tolle, Jack Vogel, Wes Gray (Alpha Architects), and Jeremy Schwartz (WisdomTree), partly because I believe in the investment theses of the products, but also because they are my friends.

not what you wish them to be, it's often because your priorities are misplaced. You don't have your purposes in order.

Focusing on your purposes means that there will be no one-size-fits-all financial or life plans. Ginny had a wonderful college experience. My parents couldn't afford to send me to college. Those past events informed our planning choices as parents.

When our children were old enough for college, providing for their education was a huge priority for Ginny and me, albeit for different reasons. Doing so cost a lot of money, money that many excellent financial planners say would be better spent on retirement planning. However, it was more important to us to provide college for them and allow them to graduate debt-free.* Because we had considered our whys, we willingly accepted the risk that we might have to work longer and make do with less in retirement.

Mimi died two days after her birthday, once eager to love and be loved, then only to be loved and remembered. Those loving remembrances are her best legacy. Mimi's cottage remains in the family. Because it is no longer big enough for everybody, Ginny and I bought our own cottage, five minutes away, that fall.

Because we live in Southern California and have owned our home for the 25 years we have lived there, we are already overweighted in real estate. The "new" cottage adds to the overweighting. Property taxes are high. It requires significant upkeep because the winters are hard and the buildings old. It's only useable in the summer and cannot practically be upgraded for year-round use. Doing so would turn us into local residents for state income tax purposes, without offset for taxes paid to our state of actual residence, because the cottage would be deemed a "permanent place of abode" pursuant to New York law no matter how little time we might spend there.

---

* Many millennials are struggling to fund the future while paying off their past. Education spending—largely on student loan debt—has become the chief financial disruptor among Americans. Shockingly, 16% of millennials have $50,000 or more in debt.

It's a lousy investment.

Ginny will be at the new cottage with our grandchildren for six weeks this summer. Their parents and I will be there a lot, too. They will play in the lake and in the sand. They will jump off the dock and the raft. They will paddle canoes, waterski, have picnics, pick blueberries, and eat s'mores. We'll put up a tetherball pole. Grace, love, and fun will abound. They will have the best time of their lives... until the next summer.

It's the most important financial investment we'll ever make.

When I was 17 and a graduating high school senior, about to go the Adirondacks for the first time and meet the love of my life, Harry Chapin had a number one hit with his haunting story-song, "Cat's in the Cradle." Chapin's lyrics recall his son wanting his time and attention without getting it before moving to a present where he wants time with his son and can't get it.

"And as I hung up the phone it occurred to me
He'd grown up just like me
My boy was just like me

"And the cat's in the cradle and the silver spoon
Little boy blue and the man in the moon
When you comin' home son
I don't know when, but we'll get together then, Dad
We're gonna have a good time then"

Chapin admitted the song scared him to death. Me too. That fear is part of why we bought the cottage. But it was love even more.

Like compound interest, success is sequential. It takes time for good choices to add up before exploding exponentially. All the best things in our lives provide benefits that compound. Our financial investments do that, and so do our personal and family investments.

Generosity and service compound. So do healthy living and education. Love is the most powerful compounder of all.

Focus your purposes there.

We don't completely control our destinies or our legacies. But if we invest well—financially and otherwise—our legacies can be profound. Mimi had her whys in order. She and Pop knew what was important to them and they invested to bring those purposes to life. Ginny and I are trying to do the same thing.

As investments need to be benchmarked, our lives need it too. No matter what we say, we show what we love by how we invest our time, our talents, and our treasure. We reveal our whys with our love. Our purposes provide benchmarks.

Ginny and I have tried to work out how we want to love and live and how we want to be remembered. We want to live on purpose. I hope you do too.

Carolyn McClanahan

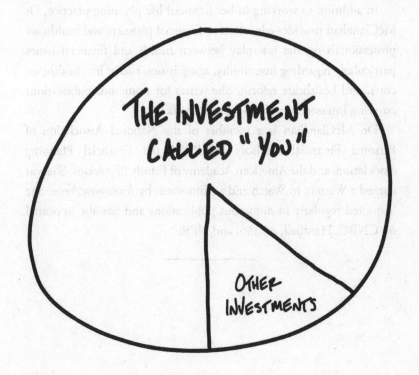

THE INVESTMENT CALLED "YOU"

OTHER INVESTMENTS

Carolyn McClanahan, M.D., CFP® is a physician and financial planner. She is the founder of Life Planning Partners, Inc., a comprehensive fee-only financial planning company.

In addition to working in her financial life planning practice, Dr. McClanahan provides education to financial planners and healthcare professionals on the interplay between health and financial issues, particularly regarding insurability, aging issues, end of life, healthcare costs, and healthcare reform. She writes for numerous publications covering intersections of money and medicine.

Dr. McClanahan is a member of the National Association of Personal Financial Advisors (NAPFA,) the Financial Planning Association, and the American Academy of Family Physicians. She was named a Woman to Watch and an Innovator by *InvestmentNews*. She is quoted regularly in numerous publications and has also appeared on CNBC, Hardball, AC360, and NPR.

THE CONCEPT OF investing and saving isn't something I learned until my late-20s. Our family didn't have money to invest. Thankfully, I was taught to invest in myself.

My dad and mom were good blue-collar working-class people who didn't have a high school education. My dad's safety net was his small Navy pension that started when he was 38 years old, when I was only six years old. His encore career as a baker entailed working 364 nights a year in his own donut shop.

We were never hungry and I never felt like we were poor. The only conversations we had about money were about budgeting—you couldn't spend more than you made. And they made it clear my sisters and I would have to find our own way when we turned 18 years old—whether that be getting married, joining the military, or going to college.

One gift my parents gave me was the ability to earn money from a young age. My dad paid me to work in the donut shop, and my seven-year-old self stood on a stool to wait on customers. I learned to do math in my head and amazed the customers with how fast I could add up the price of their donuts. They gave me big tips and nicknamed me "The Human Calculator." I didn't save any of that money—it all went for the frivolities of youth that my parents couldn't afford.

Another gift my family gave me early on was the joy of reading. Because of that, I did well in school and my teachers told me I was smart enough to go to college. Fortunately, I received a full academic scholarship to Mississippi University for Women—attending that institution was one of the smartest decisions of my life. My family would send me spending money, and I worked various jobs to add to the pot. Of course, I didn't save a dime.

My admission to medical school was a huge deal and I had to figure out a way to afford it. Out of the blue, I was awarded a full scholarship for my first year of medical school. Why? The National Health Service provided scholarships to the poorest male and female in the class and I made the cut. Wow! I had no idea we were that poor.

In residency in the early '90s is when I learned about investing. Everyone was into "hot stocks" and trying to beat the market. I made small investments in an IRA and joined the fray of stock pickers. I read Peter Lynch, Value Line, and anything else I could find the time to fit in.

I met my future husband in 1996. He was an engineer, an only child, and his parents had recently died and he received an inheritance. Not enough for a 35-year-old engineer to retire on, but enough to provide flexibility. I helped him invest that money and we did well. Little did I know—we were just lucky.

By 1999, I thought I knew it all. In addition to practicing emergency medicine, I day traded stocks on the side. That didn't last long—taking care of heart attacks and dying people was much less stressful than day trading. I lost a fair amount of money but thankfully it wasn't close to enough to put my husband's pot of money at risk. And we paid off our mortgage, so that was a nice safety net and decrease in cash outflows.

It was in 2000 that my husband and I tried to find a financial planner. We wanted to make sure he had enough money to no longer go back to engineering—he wanted to be a track coach and photographer. I was happy practicing medicine and didn't want to support him. Our goal was to find someone to tell us whether this was possible.

All the advisors we interviewed were only interested in investments and sold high-priced products. They didn't do real financial planning. It was then I went back to school for fun to learn about financial planning and fell in love with it. A nice side effect? I learned the most important determinant of financial independence was not how much you save—it is how much you spend.

In 2002, I cut my medical practice to part-time to learn more about financial planning and explore it as a career. My husband and I also cut out all the wasteful spending and we easily lived on my part-time income and kept his pot of money intact. This allowed me to start my financial planning practice in 2004. In 2005, I gave up practicing medicine for money.

Those early years in my practice were lean. I wanted to learn how to be a great financial planner and reinvested in my business. We continued to live well and frugally, and to this day, our spending is about what we value in life—experience, charity, and convenience. There is not much outlay for consumer goods so we don't have the upkeep costs of expensive toys and real estate.

I love my work and we are mainly saving for the day I can't work. We maximize our retirement plans and save as if my business will have zero value when I quit. Since we don't have children, anything left over when we die goes to charity.

So what about investing? After my day trading fiasco, I became a convert of diversification and investing for the long term. At that point in my life, I still thought people were smart enough to beat the market, so I used actively traded funds and was attracted to "bear market funds" that would provide protection in a downturn.

From 2004 to 2007, I explored alternative investments and decided they weren't worth the risk. The due diligence, lack of transparency, and spotty records were off-putting. My time was much better spent on doing great financial planning. During that time period, I also investigated the passive/active debate and gradually eased myself and my clients into more passive funds—about half and half. I wasn't convinced that one was better than the other.

2009 threw me over the fence into the passive camp. Why? All those great "bear market funds" tanked worse than the rest! At that same time, my practice was big enough to hire my first professional employee to do what I didn't love—manage investments. Tim Utech is a CFA, and managed active large cap mutual funds before switching to personal finance. His one request to come and work for me is that I had to throw myself wholly into the passive camp. And so I did.

My other belief that I'm sometimes on the fence about is individual bonds versus bond funds. Our clients are high net worth and we use mostly individual bonds to fill the fixed income side of their portfolio. Why? I like the known cash flows and capital preservation. We hold bonds to maturity and don't have to worry about the interest rate fluctuations. Tim does a great job explaining to the clients how bonds work and they are happy with the approach. Yes, it is more work, but we have plenty of good bond dealers and Tim makes sure we get good pricing.

Tim now manages my and my husband's money according to our investment policy statement. The allocation is 50% fixed income and 50% equities, and we use all the same funds as our clients. I look at the balances periodically but couldn't tell you our exact holdings to save my life. We just keep socking money away and track our spending year to year. We know we are plenty fine for the day I can no longer work.

My biggest takeaway for everyone is what my parents taught me—invest in yourself. Your ability to work is your safest and highest returning asset. By lifelong learning, and taking care of your physical health, mental health, and relationships, you are much more likely to lead a secure and satisfying life without regrets. Isn't that what it is all about?

Tyrone Ross

MISTAKES → LEARNING → LEGACY!

Tyrone Ross is a financial consultant, founder of 401stc, and Director of Community at Altruist where he also hosts the Human Advisor Podcast. He is a graduate of Seton Hall University, and was also a 2004 Olympic Trials qualifier in track and field in the 400 meters. He was recognized by *InvestmentNews* 40 under 40 (2019), and WealthManagement.com as a top ten advisor set to change the industry in 2019. FinancialPlanning.com named him as one of 20 people who will change wealth management in 2020. Tyrone is a proud first generation high school graduate whose life's mission is to be a voice for the voiceless. He is passionate about financial literacy, ending childhood hunger, homelessness, and poverty. He currently resides in Woodbridge, NJ.

I GREW UP in a financially illiterate home which dealt some hard financial lessons. At times we were unbanked and at others underbanked thanks to check cashing places. Scratch off tickets saved us plenty of days when money was short, which is why to this day I find it hard to curse the lottery. I was 26 before I knew that the stock market even existed. This wasn't for lack of exposure, I guess. When I was in college I had a teammate that used to watch these green and red numbers float across the bottom of the TV screen before practice. I used to laugh at him (he went on to become treasurer of Disney) and beg him to come chase girls with me.

Years later I would walk on to Wall Street having never taken a business, economics, accounting, or finance class. I only got a job after having an answer (that I still don't remember) for the ridiculous question of, "How will being a probation officer help you on Wall Street?" Now imagine being a 26-year-old, financially illiterate black male sitting in the epicenter of capital markets and having to answer that question. It was then and over the last 14 years that I've learned everything I know about money, saving, and investing. Along the way I've made every financial mistake imaginable, but I was privileged to be working in an industry that would expose my ignorance and accelerate my knowledge.

I don't have the quintessential "my first stock" story, but I recall learning what a 401(k) was shortly after starting my first Wall Street job. (I later emptied out that account to waste it on living expenses.)

At that time it was simply the latest in a series of stupid financial moves anyone who comes from my background could relate to. Buying lots of gaudy jewelry, a nice car, destroying my credit, and spending everything I made ad infinitum. I was working in finance, yet oblivious to the access I had to begin to secure financial freedom for my family and I. The irony of that is not lost on me to this day. The juxtaposition of working on Wall Street while oblivious to the difference between buy side and sell side was not an experience many amongst me shared.

I'd eventually move on to a brokerage "chop shop" where I learned more about stocks due to having to pitch them over the phone all day. Little did I know I'd eventually use that knowledge after securing my next job in an advisor trainee position at Merrill Lynch. It was there that I finally appreciated what it meant to be an investor. I started to manage my own 401(k), loaded up on Bank of America stock, and (because I needed the business for my goals) sold myself a VUL whole life policy. "Financial planning" also became part of my vocabulary as I began to work with wealthy families and experienced how they made, grew, transferred, and protected their wealth.

I left Merrill to go independent in 2017 after learning about Bitcoin in 2015 and working with startup founders in 2016. This is important because now the majority of my investments are tied up in cryptoassets and the equity of private companies. I do own a few stocks here and there, put money away in retirement accounts, and recently opened an HSA. I also recently became a business owner after realizing and then learning the wealth-building power of ownership.

If it wasn't apparent after reading all of that, yes, I'm a single man. I'm afforded the ability to take on an abnormal amount of risk as I try to make up for the lost time that I knew nothing of investing.

I think the most important lesson I've learned over the last 14 years as I've grown into being an investor is the importance of leaving a legacy. When you come from humble beginnings, and you are blessed enough to acquire financial knowledge, it's important to pass it on. I've made it my life's mission to use my experiences, access and privilege to help others and provide a blueprint for "illiteracy to legacy". This is why my best "investment" to date is the Tyrone Ross Jr. Athletic Endowment Fund at Georgia Tech. I was kicked out of the school (not too long after becoming the first high school graduate in my family) after opening my first bank account as an 18-year-old at a bank right off of campus.

I guess I can sum up my investing history with: failure pays the best interest.

Dasarte Yarnway

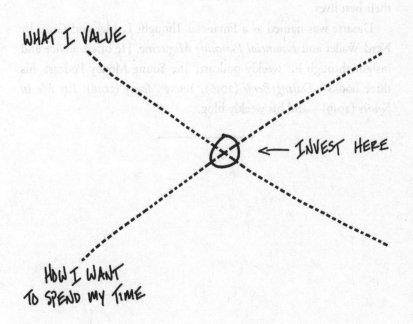

WHAT I VALUE

INVEST HERE

HOW I WANT
TO SPEND MY TIME

Dasarte Yarnway is the Founder & Managing Director of Berknell Financial Group, an innovative independent wealth management firm focused on helping millennials and seasoned investors design their best lives.

Dasarte was named as a Financial Thought Leader and Guru by Nerd Wallet and *Financial Planning Magazine*. He offers advice and insight through his weekly podcast, The Young Money Podcast, his three books—*Dating Benji* (2016), *Young Money* (2018), *Pay Me In Equity* (2019)—and his weekly blog.

MONEY, AND HOW we invest it, is just an extension of who we are. The truth behind money is that it is an outward expression of our DNA. Most of who we are and what we value can be traced through how we decide to invest our dollars.

I am a first-generation Liberian-American man, born to parents who fled their homeland before a deadly civil war. We were not rich in dollars, but rich in love, experiences and the unwavering belief that all that we had is all that we needed. We were grateful, resourceful and giving to those in our community, although there was little to spare. I've experienced devastating loss, repeatedly, and these events have conditioned me to value time because my reality has helped me to see that this precious resource is finite.

These characteristics are interwoven in the way that I invest my money. I'm a young man, all of 29 years old. Like most in this accumulation phase of life, time is my biggest asset. Before money, I know that how I invest my time will consequentially manifest in wealth—including, but not limited to—cash. The intersection of my time and values provides a compass for how I should invest my dollars. To be clear: If I *value* a particular thing, person or place, I want to invest my money there. If I am also spending a significant amount of *time* on said thing, person or place, I also will consider investing there. As a bonus, if something buys back time, I'll certainly invest my money there, because then I can reinvest the free time on more of what I value. I consider this a part of my personal investment policy statement.

Now, to the money. Most of my net worth is tied to my business, Berknell Financial Group, that I founded in 2015 after working for larger financial services companies. I started this company with nothing but a dollar and a dream. As the sole equity owner, my investment in Berknell does three things. The first: It allows me to own my time. My dad never saw me play a youth, or college football game. Even before he fell ill with cancer, he was working multiple jobs to make sure that my mother, siblings and I had all that we needed. By being a business owner, I believe that I have the opportunity to never miss one of life's precious moments. The equity in time means being physically present for experiences that you cannot buy in currency. I imagine my future wife saying that I always made time for her. My future daughter enjoying our dates. My son and I getting haircuts together and talking about life, manhood and responsibility. These are moments that I look forward to, especially because they were so short-lived for me.

The second thing my firm does is that it gives me the chance to be a servant-leader. If you want to judge the character of a man, judge not his words but his actions. Through this business, I get to *do*. I can show people what it means to commit to something, teach people how to design their own wealth, and motivate people to lean into their God-given abilities and their calling. Seeing people prosper through these actions is the biggest rate of return.

Lastly, I get to create a legacy. What are people saying about you when you are not in the room? What will they say about you when you are gone? Members of the Liberian community of Northern California called my father, "The Godfather," because he saved more than 45 refugees from their war-stricken homeland. He'd go out of his way to serve their kids, as if they were his own. I have many "brothers" and "sisters" with whom there are no biological ties, but because one man decided it was worth his time and money to invest in them, our bond is unbreakable. Through the company, and all of the small acts of selflessness and courage, I *will* create a legacy that will not only be calculable by numbers.

For this reason, I continue to invest my money in the creation of businesses that will offer similar impacts. The most recent of which is the Ganta Real Estate Company. In this project, I plan on redeveloping neighborhoods that were to be gentrified and providing affordable housing to those who would otherwise be forced out due to the increasing costs and demand. Ganta Real Estate Company's namesake is a northeastern city in Liberia, near the birthplace of my dad. The Gio and Mano tribes that inhabited the region were known to be extremely progressive and skilled warriors. The company has these same underlying principles. Through this, I task myself and my partners to protect and serve those who may not be able to do so for themselves.

As for more traditional investments, I have a SEP IRA that I use as a part of my tax strategy and for retirement planning. I align my portfolio with the investments of my clients. Through volatile markets, I believe that there is power in being able to tell someone that's trusting in me that I am invested right alongside them. This provides a deeper layer of trust. Roughly 25% of this account is invested in individual equities—particularly in companies that align with my values, or through fundamental analysis that I believe will withstand the test of time. Some are speculative, some aggressive, and a good chunk are proven companies with dividends. I love individual stocks because I believe that here is where premium returns are made, if and only if, you have the stomach for the inevitable volatility. The larger bulk of my investments are comprised of exchange traded funds. I refer to this portion as my "core portfolio." Systematically, I contribute to this concentrated set of funds and rebalance two times per year on average. I have an individual taxable account, and a trust that I seek to invest more into as my earnings increase, which they have every year since the inception of my business.

Coming from larger firms, I was conditioned to think that the traditional way of investing was the only way, but the more that I expand my knowledge and client pool, I'm seeing that it is not. While the bulk of my money is poured into my business, my family and the things that I value, I take pride in investing in people. Whenever I see an entrepreneur who, like me, has bootstrapped, is creative or simply is moving forward along his or her journey, I take the time to figure out how I can support. This may be through buying their books, music, or a ticket to a paid event. I believe that success leaves fingerprints, and without these initial "investors" I doubt that I would still be running my business today. By investing in people in the smallest ways, you can realize the biggest alpha.

Overall, my investment philosophy is a disciplined, people-centered strategy that is an extension of my heart and entrepreneurial spirit. I believe that by investing in this way, not only will I sow the seeds for a fruitful harvest, but I can change the world along the way. If our strategies only center around us, we've missed our one chance to permeate the most important things in life: love, faith, joy, good health and the bond of community. After this, all else are non-essential.

It is my hope that investors expand their minds and create room in their investment policy statement to be agents of change for a better world. Together, we can.

Nina O'Neal

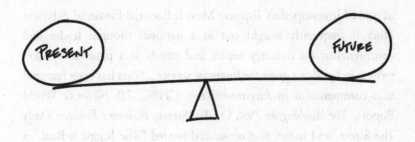

A financial services professional since 2004, Nina O'Neal is an industry veteran. Currently she is a Partner and Investment Advisor with Archer Investment Management. Nina has been named one of the *InvestmentNews* 40 under 40 Financial Professionals as well as one of Investopedia's Top 100 Most Influential Financial Advisors. Nina is frequently sought out as a national thought leader and commentator on industry topics and trends as a panelist, speaker, writer, and podcast guest for financial services. Nina has been featured as a commentator in *InvestmentNews*, CNBC, US News & World Report, *The Washington Post*, OnWallStreet, *Investor's Business Daily*, The Street, and more. She wrote and hosted "The Juggle is Real," a video series with *InvestmentNews* that shares the unique challenges of working parents. Nina is a graduate of the University of North Carolina at Chapel Hill. Her passions are watching her two young sons play baseball, trying new restaurants, traveling, and reading.

I HAVE ALWAYS had a love/hate relationship with money. As a child in North Carolina, I recall money being stressful, especially after my parents got divorced around the time I was finishing elementary school. I grew up in a world where most of my family were small business owners, so cash flow problems were hardly foreign to them. My childhood, it seemed, was a never-ending rollercoaster of "have" or "have-not." Financial stability never seemed to find it's way to my home.

By the time I was in high school, I worked multiple jobs in order to have my own money. It meant freedom, the chance to buy the things and have the experiences that I wanted for my life. As a teenager, I vowed never to be financially dependent upon anyone. I swore to work hard to make a great career that could provide a lifestyle that I dreamt I wanted for myself and one day for my family.

Despite my unstable experience with family finances, I still managed to find the stock market fascinating. Growing up, I would sit with my grandfather and review the stock market pages in the local newspaper. With the advent of the internet and online brokerages, I even began helping my grandfather and the owner of a local company that I worked for purchase stocks in E*Trade accounts based on my research of the companies. I created a mock Yahoo! portfolio which I enjoyed following, tracking whether my "investments" did well (or not). Trading stocks seemed so disconnected from my day-to-day interactions with real money. As a teenager, it just seemed like a fun game. Little did I know how much that opinion would change, drastically, just a few years later.

After graduating from college, I moved to New York City. In high school we took a field trip to New York, and I dreamed since then of living there. The terrorist attacks of September 11th happened when I was in college. The people of New York coming together during and afterward moved me. I wanted to be part of something like that.

So, young and naive, I moved to the city and landed an entry-level PR job in the fashion industry. This was 2003, it paid $33,000 per year, and I was living in Manhattan. After taxes, my rent was more than two weeks' worth of paychecks! Still, I loved New York, despite the cost. Unfortunately, I spent the next year and a half racking up credit card debt. I struggled with budgeting and the cost of living in the city. I was also 22 years old having the time of my life, so it was easy to think that I would deal with the debt later. When anyone asked me to do anything socially, my answer was always yes. I knew that I would not live in Manhattan forever, so I wanted to make the most of the experience there. Unfortunately that came with a cost.

With some encouragement from friends in finance, I pivoted careers to Wall Street. I had many friends that worked in financial services. Their jobs and the way all of the players on Wall Street interacted really fascinated me. I was constantly asking them questions and finally decided to contact a recruiter to see if there was an opportunity for me. Eagerly, I accepted an offer to work at an institutional money manager. At this firm I learned so much: corporate finance, disciplined investing, the importance of relationships with clients—all valuable.

As a result, I began to turn around my own finances; not just because I was making more money, but also I had a better grasp of understanding personal financial fundamentals. It felt good to see savings increase, debt decrease, investments in a 401(k), and better control over my cash flow. After a short time with this firm, I moved back home and took an opportunity as a financial advisor with Merrill

Lynch. I realized that I had a fire for helping people understand financial concepts and personal financial planning. I still do.

We are the sum of our experiences, and my path from North Carolina to New York and back again has shaped how I now manage my own money. However, the stock market long ago stopped being a fun game that has no connection to day-to-day financials. Now, I view the stock market as an incredible tool for reaching long-term financial goals that requires careful management and a highly disciplined approach to investing. As a financial advisor, I am able to benefit from professional training and personal experiences to navigate my finances.

To expand, let me share my family and business dynamics. During the financial crisis, my training program at Merrill Lynch was terminated, which seemed like the end of my career as an advisor. In hindsight, this gave me a unique opportunity as I was able to carefully and intentionally decide what my next step would be.

Unemployment was also a valuable financial lesson to learn as a newly married couple. During this time my current business partner and I ran into each other, and we had a quick conversation that changed my life. He encouraged me to not only continue my passion for financial planning and investing but to do so as his business partner. Today we co-own a boutique financial planning and investment management company that helps hundreds of clients across the country.

An entrepreneur as well, my husband owns a creative agency that provides creative direction, art, illustration, package design, and brand design. As with most people in the creative space, his income fluctuates with each year. We have two boys, ages 5 and 8 years old. Evidently, kids are expensive.

Now, in my late 30s, my main financial concerns are cash flow (self-employment), taxes (did I mention self-employment), college savings, private school tuition, and retirement savings. Taxes and tuition periodically require large cash payments. I utilize multiple accounts at Capital One 360, each labeled with a unique purpose such as taxes, tuition, general savings, etc. Each month for the larger cash needs account with specific purposes, I contribute whatever amount that I am comfortable with at that time. It could be fully funding or a small amount. It depends on the income received and upcoming cash needs. Also, as a very visual person, it is helpful to see the funds separately.

My husband and I decided when our kids were very young that we would invest in a private school education for them. This can be a controversial topic with judgments cutting both ways. I guess what I'd say is it's a very personal decision and to each their own. Without divulging specifics about my oldest son, we felt very early on that he would benefit from a small classroom and other things that a private school could provide. The financial commitment to fund two children in a private school is significant. Yet it has been one of our greatest investments so far, one with huge, obvious benefits for their education and overall development. We will take it year by year to determine if we keep on this path.

Beyond our large annual cash needs, we also save for future financial needs for mid-term savings, retirement, and college education. These are the accounts that are invested in the market. Each month we have established an automated draft to our joint brokerage account from our joint checking account. If all of our other cash needs are met, some of the excess cash available is invested into a joint brokerage account. For example, if taxes and tuition or any other large cash payments have already been completed, then I would determine what excess cash reserves could be moved to our joint brokerage account.

There are different philosophies with financial advisors on how they invest, but I prefer not to invest my own accounts and do not purchase securities for my own accounts. Therefore, I utilize third-party money managers to manage my brokerage account to their specific strategy. I tend to be pretty aggressive and like the benefit of dollar-cost-averaging through monthly contributions. I prefer to invest in mutual funds and exchange traded funds.

When each of my children was born, I immediately established a John Hancock 529 College Savings Account. I have the accounts set up for automatic monthly contributions, plus occasional gifts from grandparents are also deposited. Within the 529 plans, I opted to allocate to aggressive growth mutual funds, since my children are so young. The benefits of dollar cost averaging, time in the market, and tax-deferred growth should help to provide ample savings for college. In the case there's a shortfall, their college can be funded by income, scholarships, and/or student loans. Currently my college savings projection for my children is only to fund a four-year in-state public school.

Saving for retirement as a small business owner is challenging. There are multiple options, but the IRS puts many restrictions around the types of accounts we are able to utilize as well as limits to contributions. I have utilized for myself SEP IRA and SIMPLE IRA accounts. Currently our company offers a SIMPLE IRA plan as the retirement benefit, and I defer money into the account with each pay period. These funds are also managed by a third-party money manager in all equity-based mutual funds and exchange traded funds.

My biggest investment is the business that I co-own. For the past 11 years, my partner and I have invested back into our financial planning and investment management company in many ways, including technology, people, office space, continuing education, and more. We've committed to keep the business debt-free and cash flow positive while providing our clients the best service and experience that we can. This was really hard to do in the early years seeing as how it cut into both of our incomes. It's been worth it. We continue to see the return on investment through client retention and acquisition that keeps us continually profitable.

The biggest return on investment is my happiness and the ability to love what I do without a corporate agenda or sales goals. Simply put, our focus is our clients. Over the years we have intentionally established wonderful relationships with people that we genuinely enjoy working with year over year.

My financial goals are not built on big returns or grandiose dreams. They anchor on financial stability and living a fulfilling life. That means the ability to do the things that we love, like traveling and experiencing new places, while also being able to comfortably provide a nice home, meet my children's educational needs, and save for the future. None of us know how long we have in this world with those that we love. Whether it is too short or very long, we have to prepare to live well both in the present and in the future.

Debbie Freeman

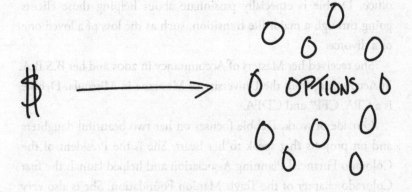

Debbie Freeman

Debbie Freeman is a Principal and Director of Financial Planning for Peak Financial Advisors in Denver, Colorado. She started with the firm in 2005 as a junior planner and tax advisor. Prior to joining Peak, Debbie worked for Deloitte Tax as a staff accountant in the Denver office. Debbie is especially passionate about helping those clients going through a major life transition, such as the loss of a loved one or a divorce.

She received her Masters of Accountancy in 2005 and her B.S.B.A. in Accounting from the University of Montana in Missoula. Debbie is a CPA, CFP® and CDFA.

Outside of work, Debbie focuses on her two beautiful daughters and on projects that speak to her heart. She is the President of the Colorado Financial Planning Association and helped launch the first Colorado chapter of the Travis Manion Foundation. She is also very passionate about veterans' issues and suicide prevention.

I WAS RAISED 2,035 miles from Wall Street. My parents are included in the 45% of Americans who do not own stocks. Witnessing their struggles and sacrifices was not always easy, but it ignited a permanent desire in me to have options. I learned early that it is almost impossible to plan for the future when you are bogged down with worries of today. Ultimately, these lessons became the foundation of my relationship with money and have shaped how I invest.

I have never been afraid of debt when used wisely. The local bank loaned me $5,500 for my first car in high school. Student loans funded my higher education. Debt is what gave me the first glimpse of independence. I had a car, an acceptance letter and a way to pay for it. This is not to say that I did not make mistakes with debt along the way, but I certainly learned quickly.

I still use debt responsibly. I have a mortgage on my home, and I have a student loan payment. The student loan is at 1.74% interest, so I have never had any desire to pay it off early. I view my education as the greatest investment I could have made in myself. The ROI on that decision has been immeasurable. The mortgage is at 3.375%, but the after-tax cost is lower. My mortgage is less than I would pay in rent and I have participated in the booming Denver real estate market for the last 13 years. I view my home as an investment in sacred family time and my sanctuary away from the rest of the world. Taking advantage of financial opportunities when they present themselves, in this case with low interest rates for both my home and education, has been at the core of building my financial independence.

I have a Roth IRA where I invest in individual equities. I typically buy companies I understand and use in my own life. I am part of a powerful demographic: the working mother. You can bet that working moms have found the longest lasting, most efficient products out there. I choose to own individual equities in this account because the potential upside will never be taxed. Asset location is one of those tools that we can use and control.

My first experience with stock picking happened in high school. I was a 15-year-old server in a coffee shop on weekend mornings. I loved that job. People are the friendliest around breakfast time. One of my regulars, Roy, would come in every weekend with a paper in hand. He would tell me stories about growing up in Montana, then moving on and seeing the world from his home base in California. He recognized that I wanted to experience more than my small town. Each weekend, he would have me choose a stock from the newspaper. I had to look up the quote, research the company during the week, report back to him the next weekend and check the stock price again. He loved seeing what stocks I would choose. I thought it was just a fun game, but he nurtured my interest in finance. I credit Roy for helping me ultimately choose my profession as a financial planner. I wrote to him after receiving my master's degree and thanked him. Each time I add a new stock to my Roth IRA, I think of Roy.

I also have a SIMPLE IRA. This is invested in the models we create for our clients. This is ingrained in my culture at the firm and I would not hire someone to manage my money if they did not invest at least some of their own money the same way. I contribute every month and my firm has a match. It is a mixture of ETFs and mutual funds, and we are active in adjusting the allocation. I invest every month, regardless of market conditions. I know I will be rewarded for starting young and allowing compound interest to work in my favor.

My SIMPLE IRA is not sexy or worth talking about at dinner. It does, however, provide intangible benefits beyond saving for the future. I am so privileged to get the opportunity to participate in a company plan. I am grateful I can afford to contribute every month. I wonder how my parents would have felt if they had been able to save anything for retirement. Better yet, what if they had worked at a job that even offered a retirement plan and an employer match? This boring account is much more than a monthly deposit. To me, it holds the promise of choice tomorrow and provides a sense of well-being and gratitude today.

The largest component of my savings (usually around 10% of my pay) goes into an online savings account. This funds my annual equity purchase with the firm. I have to admit, this can be difficult some months. I am a divorced mom, building a life for myself and my girls. Putting aside this much, especially with after-tax dollars, can be a struggle. I feel pride each year when I write that check. This is an investment in me. This is an investment in the success of my clients. Every dollar of that buy-in shows my daughters that women not only belong in finance but that we can thrive in it.

Recognizing that higher education was the greatest investment I ever made, I opened 529 plans for both of my girls when they were infants. Those are managed by Vanguard and I contribute monthly. It is unlikely I will save enough to cover all their higher education needs, but I am at peace with it. It feels right to me personally to have them contribute in some way. Even if my financial situation changed substantially, I would still like them to approach college with some skin in the game.

The last component of my savings and investing habits is my absolute favorite. It is my monthly deposit into an online savings account exclusively for a dream vacation when I turn 40. I am just like many of you; big plans to live the life we crave take discipline and planning. However, many people do not commit to getting it done. Not me. Not anymore.

You see, I lost my brother to suicide in 2014. Although this experience has been unimaginable, you go through a tremendous amount of growth and evolution after these types of events. One thing I realized was I had spent the first 34 years of my life doing everything I was supposed to do. I studied hard in college. I have worked hard my entire life. I got married and had babies just like I was raised to believe I should do. What I did not do was take time to grow through travel and adventure. I didn't spend spring breaks in Mexico or travel extensively before having kids.

Some of that was limited by budget, but it was also limited by this duty to follow the expected course. Losing Joe was a true awakening. It taught me that life is not just about the next big milestone. It is also about enjoying the moments in between. So I save for those experiences I want to do now: summer vacations with family in Montana, Hawaii at 40, Paris when my oldest turns 16, Everest basecamp when my daughters are in their 20s. I'll never get there without making it a priority with disciplined savings.

We all have a different roadmap for investing. I have always approached my investments like I approach life. It takes effort and the acceptance of risk to change your circumstances. Be willing to act when financial opportunities present themselves. Be consistent and disciplined with your long-term goals, but do not get so fixated on the future that you forget to enjoy today. Keep a positive perspective and trust your instincts. Finally, never underestimate how fortunate we are to have these choices. Having options and a little bit of luck are the key to financial security.

"You have exactly one life in which to do everything you will ever do. Act accordingly." —Colin Wright

Shirl Penney

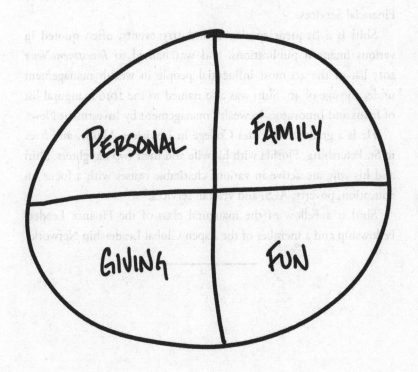

Shirl Penney is the founder, President, and CEO of Dynasty Financial Partners. Prior to Dynasty, Shirl worked at Citi Smith Barney as Director of Private Wealth Management and Head of Executive Financial Services.

Shirl is a frequent speaker at industry events, often quoted in various financial publications, and was named to *InvestmentNews'* 2015 list of the 40 most influential people in wealth management under the age of 40. Shirl was also named to the 2016 inaugural list of Icons and Innovators in wealth management by Investment News.

He is a graduate of Bates College in Lewiston, Maine, and lives in St. Petersburg, Florida with his wife and their two daughters. Shirl and his wife are active in various charitable causes with a focus on education, poverty, ALS, and veteran services.

Shirl is a Fellow of the inaugural class of the Finance Leaders Fellowship and a member of the Aspen Global Leadership Network.

F OR SOMEONE WHO had a rocky financial start in my youth—
growing up very poor in the sticks of Maine raised by my step-
grandfather, where for a period of time when I was aged 11 to 14 I was
homeless and lived with various neighbors—it's humbling to be asked
now at age 43 how I invest my money!

This year will mark the 10-year anniversary since I founded Dynasty
Financial Partners; a middle office platform services, investment
product, and capital provider for top independent wealth managers
(RIAs), which now is approaching nearly $50 billion in assets on the
platform. Like many founders or entrepreneurs still actively engaged
in running their businesses, I am the President and CEO of Dynasty,
and a substantial portion of my net worth is still riding alongside the
other equity owners and partners at the firm.

While I acknowledge that sometimes the "all in" mentality of
entrepreneurs can be risky versus more aggressively diversifying
overtime, thankfully the bet on the business, the strategy, industry,
our people, and our clients has paid off nicely thus far.

That said, my wife Mary Ann and I do have other investments.
By describing these I can give you a sense of how we think about our
overall approach to deploying our capital around our concentration
in Dynasty Financial Partners LLC.

We have four broad categories or pools of capital as we think about
it. They are personal capital (Mary Ann and myself), family capital
(our two daughters and nieces and nephews, etc.), philanthropic

Capital (we focus on education, ALS, and helping military families), and our "fun" capital bucket (assets we like to enjoy but where we are not fixated on financial return).

With our personal capital Mary Ann and I are still fairly young, and thankfully healthy, so we have a fairly aggressive growth portfolio. We invest in a diversified portfolio consisting of index funds in the core part of portfolio, managed money for small cap and international, and currently have a 10% allocation to both fixed income and cash.

I am a believer in investing in things you know with people you know. In the past that drove us to buying other finance stocks of companies that were run by people I knew and respected. Given the size of our closely held position in Dynasty today, and that it's a financial services company, I have stopped buying other companies in the space given the concentration risk to industry sector. Of the 80% in growth investments, roughly 50% is in public markets and the other 30% is in alternative investments, split between a handful of funds in the private equity and real estate space, and direct investments in companies run by teams I believe in that are not in financial services.

The family capital pool is mostly Dynasty stock at this point, plus some individual stocks that we have allowed our girls to pick as a way of educating them on investing. The stocks are mostly names that you would expect two 11- and 13-year-old girls to be excited about owning. We love watching them present their investment ideas to us at Friday night dinners! They also have educational funds which are in aggressive, growth-oriented, diversified public equity funds.

Our philanthropic capital is invested the most conservatively of our capital pools, with domestic equity indexing in core at roughly 30%, with a high dividend value manager at 20%, 25% taxable fixed income, 15% international mutual funds, and 10% in cash. We contribute about 10% of annual income to the pool and plan to fund it at a much higher level post a potential liquidity event with Dynasty stock down the road. Both Mary Ann and I are very passionate about our giving efforts.

Our last pool of capital is the fun bucket. We refer to this as H&H: houses and horses! We have a number of personal properties that we use with our family and friends. And we have a stable of thoroughbred racehorses—oftentimes we have partnered on horses with various friends. While both the houses and the horses have a chance to provide financial returns, and we have been fortunate with both over the years, it's not the primary focus of the pool or capital.

We believe success is best when shared and when we have 50 people at one of our homes, or in the winners circle with us, you can't put a price tag on that "investment"!

Ted Seides

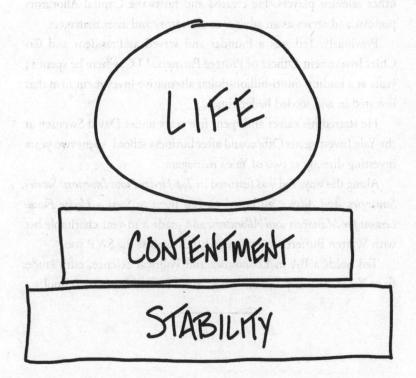

Ted Seides, CFA is the Founder of Capital Allocators LLC, which he created in 2016 to explore best practices in the asset management industry from the perspective of asset owners, asset managers, and other relevant players. He created and hosts the Capital Allocators podcast and serves as an advisor to allocators and asset managers.

Previously, Ted was a founder and served as President and Co-Chief Investment Officer of Protégé Partners, LLC, where he spent 14 years at a leading multi-billion-dollar alternative investment firm that invested in and seeded hedge funds.

He started his career and spent five years under David Swensen at the Yale Investments Office, and after business school, spent two years investing directly at two of Yale's managers.

Along the way, Ted was featured in *Top Hedge Fund Investors: Stories, Strategies, and Advice*, authored *So You Want to Start a Hedge Fund: Lessons for Managers and Allocators*, and made a 10-year charitable bet with Warren Buffett pitting hedge funds against the S&P 500.

Ted holds a BA in Economics and Political Science, cum laude, from Yale University and an MBA from Harvard Business School.

MY FORMATIVE EDUCATION in investing came from my father and my first boss, a fellow named David Swensen.

My dad lost his parents when he was in his teens and 20s. They didn't have much money, and he put himself through college and medical school. Some family friends told him about stocks when they passed away, and he bought IBM in 1959. When everything felt like it got taken away from him in an instant, he hung onto those shares. He still owns them today.

We had an upper middle class life. I thought we were rich and just told people we were middle class—I didn't know any different. We took vacations to a timeshare in the Poconos, where I skied in the winter and played tennis in the summer. My parents put my two siblings and I through college and graduate school with no debt and started each of us off in our lives with some money in the bank as well. I remember my childhood as secure, stable, and worry free, even though I wasn't surrounded by the trappings of the wealthy. Those feelings are how I describe contentment.

Money was not abundant, and it was a source of worry for my father despite my youthful impressions. He never talked about money specifically, instead offering advice such as "don't be a doctor, there are easier ways of making a living." I knew he was talking about money, and I never heard the phrase "pursue your passion" until I went to business school. Perhaps it was no surprise that I went into the money business.

The tricky part of following my father's advice was that he wasn't fully financially literate. He knew how to balance a checkbook, but I recently learned that for decades he borrowed on his credit card and brokerage margin, even though he could have swapped those debts for lower interest rate student and mortgage loans. His advice about money was directionally right and specifically unactionable.

David Swensen was like a second father to me in the five years I worked for him at Yale. We developed a part fraternal, part paternal relationship in which I thrived and which I have cherished ever since. He taught me everything about investing that my father didn't know. David also was not a lavish spender, and the basic lessons of saving for the future were apparent for me to follow.

Behind the curtain, David was every bit as effective as he appears to the public. He taught me first principles and good investment habits before I developed bad ones, and his daily wisdom about life resonated deeply with me. I clung to whatever came out of his mouth.

In the years after I left Yale, I had a successful career applying the lessons I learned from David to serve a range of institutional clients. I made mistakes along the way and found myself coming back to David's first principles with a deeper understanding each time. In the decade and a half in my business, I made a bunch of money and didn't have to think carefully about funding anything I wanted, which wasn't much.

My financial life hit a bump in the road after I left Protégé Partners. At the same time, my income dropped precipitously, I went through a divorce, and my balance sheet shrank to a fraction of what it once was. The loss of stability I had been accustomed to throughout my life shook me to the core. I was ill-prepared for it both emotionally and financially. Many people go through similar tough times, and I was more fortunate than most in that I had enough financial wherewithal to take a step back without severe consequences.

I never had a financial plan back then, and I wish I had. I found myself post-divorce with an expensive life, three kids, and a house that was difficult to sell. I had to make adjustments that I never foresaw. A financial plan and a good financial planner would have given me peace of mind and may have helped me make better decisions along the way. I still need a financial plan and have finally begun the process to create one.

All the while, contentment has meant a feeling of stability for myself and my loved ones, the fun experiences we share together, and never having to think twice about necessities. I want my kids and family to have this foundation, and I don't need much *stuff* to be happy. I've also found the love of my life and am reassessing what my future financial picture looks like in a newly constructed family.

Some of the lessons I learned as an institutional investor don't apply to funding my contentment as an individual. During my time managing hedge fund portfolios, I was restricted in what I could own and invested most of my capital alongside my clients. Those investments were wildly suboptimal for me. Hedge funds are generally tax inefficient and assume less risk than I wanted. However, it was important to signal to my clients that I was aligned with them and focused on their capital.

It took me a while to find my footing as an individual investor after I left Protégé. Once I did, here's what I found.

When my life is cash flow positive and I leave a buffer in cash to protect against lean years, I feel a sense of stability and can freely invest the remainder of my assets with a long time horizon. I'm comfortable with equity market volatility, and I don't believe in marketing timing, so I stay fully invested.

I perform best when I stick to my strengths, and I took stock of how to apply these traits as an individual investor. I'm a good contrarian buyer, a mediocre short-term trader, a reluctant seller, and a serene owner through choppy markets. I also love investing in outstanding people pursuing value-added strategies. Put that together and I found my comfort zone with investments in funds and stocks that I intend to buy and hold, hopefully for as long as my father has owned IBM.

I mostly own global equities in a mix of active and passive funds. I hold index or factor ETFs in absence of something better to do, but I much prefer active management. This bias comes from my positive experience with select active managers throughout my career.

The value of relationships goes entirely unmentioned in the active-passive debate. Partnering with active managers offers access to people, ideas, and opportunities that can never occur while investing in an index fund. The unquantifiable knowledge and optionality that accrues from these relationships are gifts that keep on giving.

Alongside funds, I invest in single stocks that fit my atypical lens on the investment world. Most of the single names in my portfolio take the form of replicating an investment in a manager. For example, in the selloff in December 2018, I bought a position in Brookfield Asset Management (BAM). I don't pretend to know more about the stock than other investors, and I don't follow their quarterly earnings reports, but I understand the company's investment strategies, its alignment with shareholders, and the fit of infrastructure and credit investments in my portfolio.

I tend to have a value bias in my manager preferences, so I own a few growth stocks to balance out the exposure. I buy stocks in companies with long runways that I'm highly confident I'll continue to own five or 10 years from now, including Amazon (AMZN), Alphabet (GOOG), and Shopify (SHOP).

I fill out my stock portfolio with a small opportunistic bucket of fliers, partly for the lure of option-like upside in dynamic sectors like biotechnology. To be fair, I know even less about these stocks than I do the others, so I invest alongside managers I know well who have done the work and have high conviction in the names.

At times, I've been allured to buy a stock I hear about from a money manager I respect that doesn't fit into one of these buckets of manager replicator, long-duration growth stock, or flier. Far too frequently, I've bought and sold the stock within a month or two, when a hint of losses made me realize I had no idea what I was doing.

For years, I imposed *stick to your knitting* on the managers I hired, and yet I need to remind myself of the same thing from time to time.

When rocky periods in the market hit like in December 2018 and March 2020, I add tax loss harvesting to my process, a wrinkle I never considered in my professional experience. It feels good to do something when markets are turbulent and swapping one ETF for a similar one and taking tax losses has given me solace in rough patches.

I certainly know my way around the hedge fund space, but I don't invest in hedge funds. I see valuable merits for outstanding hedge funds in tax-exempt institutional portfolios. As a taxable investor, it's hard to derive the benefits without the costs.

Outside of the public markets, I invest in a few private equity funds with managers pursuing unusually attractive strategies. Some of my past relationships and more recent investigations from my Capital Allocators podcast have turned up some wonderful opportunities. Fortunately, the managers were kind to offer me access.

All told, by blending a cash balance and an equity portfolio, I can achieve the stability I seek with compounding for a future of more stability, fun times, and a good life.

Ashby Daniels

ENOUGH

SATISFACTION   EXCESS

Ashby Daniels is a Financial Advisor with Shorebridge Wealth Management. He works with people at or nearing retirement and walks with them every step of the way at this critical juncture of their lives. Ashby is the author of *Medicare Simplified: What Retirees Need to Know About Medicare in 100 Pages or Less*, which is a Medicare bestseller on Amazon.

He actively writes a blog called Retirement Field Guide where he writes about investing, Social Security, Medicare and all aspects of preparing for retirement. He lives in Pittsburgh, PA with his wife and two sons.

I GREW UP in a household that didn't enjoy a lot of excess. We were beneficiaries of the free lunch program in school and we huddled in front a temporary heater on cold winter mornings. That was common around the area I grew up, so it never seemed out of place. Don't get me wrong though, we were lucky. Our needs were met and we often gave away what little excess we had to families less fortunate than us. It was obvious that caring for others was important to my parents. The older I've gotten, the more admirable I find that to be. As I imagine is true for many people, much of how I manage our family's financial life is probably defined by my childhood experiences. I believe in keeping things simple and it starts with defining *enough*.

Enough from a worldly perspective is an ever-moving target because there is always a bigger boat, bigger house, nicer car or more extravagant vacation. But enough is defined internally, not externally. For me, enough is acknowledging the line between satisfaction and excess. Thanks to my childhood, I don't require much in the way of material things to be satisfied.

I believe common excesses often complicate life rather than make it more fulfilling. As they say, I never want the things I own to end up owning me. I have never cared about expensive watches, high-end cars, having the biggest house or anything like that, so I am sure it's easier for me to come to grips with this idea than others. I believe it is healthy to have wants that go unfulfilled. We live comfortably, but anything beyond enough is to be saved or given away. We keep it simple.

Since I began my career, our household earnings have increased year over year, but we have deliberately kept our lifestyle the same. Few people discuss the impact lifestyle choices can have on their financial future, but I believe it will account for about 80% or more of our personal financial destiny. It's not going to be the fund choices or any other tactical decision that will determine our success. It will be our ability to live well below our means. Though, it cannot be done alone.

My wife and I are both fiscally conservative when it comes to our household spending. We are both avid savers and we desire to give much away to people and causes we care about. We give not only because we care about the cause we are giving to, but because it is good for our souls. We have been very lucky and believe we are called to be good stewards of what we have been blessed with.

We are not fans of debt and pay cash for just about everything, cars included. The only debt we maintain is our mortgage due to the low interest rate. I follow the same advice I have given to many clients in similar situations and haven't paid a penny more than is owed since we purchased our home ten years ago. To me, having the funds available to pay it off if we needed to is the same as the mortgage being paid off. It works for us.

We have three primary financial goals:

1. Prepare for retirement,
2. Pay for college for our two sons, and
3. Be prepared for life's what ifs.

Executing on these goals is where keeping things simple really applies. I believe people spend far too much time trying to optimize every little thing, especially their portfolios. Once something is good enough, I move on to more pressing issues.

When investing for retirement and our children's education, I will excitedly say that our portfolio is 100% equities. Some might say this is foolish and that we should own some percentage of fixed income to reduce the volatility of the portfolio, but I disagree because we have no short-term goals. It is widely accepted that anything that reduces short-term volatility must also reduce long-term return. Given this fact, it seems illogical to own anything but equities assuming we have the emotional fortitude to think truly long term. I believe we do and will continue to own 100% equities.

As for the equities we own, if I am honest—and I say this with tremendous respect and admiration for my colleagues in investment research and fund management—I believe the quest to squeak out a few extra basis points of return is a waste of time for the typical Main Street investor, myself included. Why? It's not because I believe it can't be done (it surely can), but because the quest for alpha is entirely out of my control and because it is entirely unnecessary for achieving our financial goals.

Part of keeping things simple is seeking areas where we can reduce frictions. In other words, I want to eliminate uncontrollable risks if at all possible. Attempting to beat the market must also introduce the risk of underperforming the market as well. If we don't need to beat the market to achieve our financial goals, what sense would it make to introduce the possibility of moving us further from our goals?

If our goals require beating the market, I believe we should revise our goals rather than attempt to do something that introduces other risks. Market returns should be good enough for our needs.

We invest our portfolio into a diversified mix of index funds and other than rebalancing our accounts, we do not touch them. I don't believe in continuously optimizing our portfolio because one fact most people willingly ignore is that all portfolio optimization is based exclusively on past data. That sounds obvious, but there seems to be a disconnect since our industry focuses so much on this idea.

If all investment research is based on past data (there is no other data), then any portfolio deemed "optimal" is out of date before it even begins because we are investing into the future where everything is unknown. In other words, we can't know what optimal is until the future gets here, at which point it's too late. If there are no facts about the future, why bother trying to optimize something that is entirely unoptimizable?

I believe being willing to stick to a diversified portfolio of index funds is the closest thing to an investing superpower that exists in the age of shiny object syndrome. Patience seems to be a much simpler and more satisfying road to our financial goals than always trying to find the next best thing.

We currently contribute monthly to my Roth 401(k) and our taxable account. Given our income levels, it may or may not be a smart long-term decision to choose Roth if we end up in a lower tax bracket in retirement, but I do it anyway because I don't mind paying taxes now. I care much more about what it could mean for us in the long run. The future tax bill is another potential friction I can eliminate by investing in this way. I also consider the question of whether I would rather pay taxes on the seed or on the tree? With 30-plus years of potential tax-free growth ahead of us, I prefer to pay taxes on the seed.

Our taxable account is becoming our most sizeable account. We look at it as an extension of our savings despite it being all equities. If we needed funds beyond our emergency savings, we are willing to accept the possibility that the market may be in the tank when we need it, if it means that we can position ourselves for higher probable returns for years to come.

The purpose of our taxable account is to provide for both retirement and education. We do not utilize 529 plans for education because we prefer optionality rather than tax benefits. If our sons end up joining the military, getting an unlikely scholarship or doing something entirely different, we are no worse for it and may provide for them in other ways because we can. By saving this way, we have given ourselves options.

For our third goal, preparing for life's what ifs, I am a big believer in insurance. I have enough life insurance to provide for my family in perpetuity and cover our education goals if something should happen to me. I have disability coverage to provide for my family if I am unable to work, and we have adequate liability insurance for the remaining what ifs. Insuring ourselves for what can go wrong is what allows us to invest for what can go right.

Understanding what matters most to us and what we are trying to achieve provides the guideposts for establishing our strategic and tactical plans that allow us to sleep well at night. There is no one right way to do anything financially, you must find what works for you and stick to it.

Blair duQuesnay

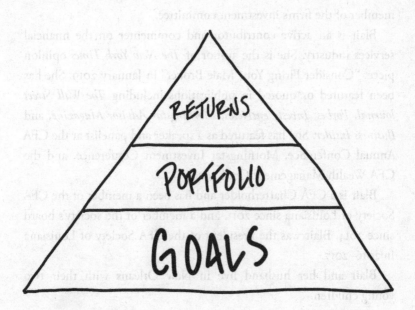

Blair duQuesnay, CFA, CFP® is an investment advisor at Ritholtz Wealth Management. She works with the firm's clients to create sustainable financial plans and investment strategies, and she is a member of the firm's investment committee.

Blair is an active contributor and commenter on the financial services industry. She is the author of *The New York Times* opinion piece, "Consider Firing Your Male Broker" in January 2019. She has been featured or quoted in publications including *The Wall Street Journal*, *Forbes*, *InvestmentNews*, *Morningstar Advisor Magazine*, and *Business Insider*. She has featured as a speaker and panelist at the CFA Annual Conference, Morningstar Investment Conference, and the CFA Wealth Management Conference.

Blair is a CFA Charterholder and has been a member of the CFA Society of Louisiana since 2011, and a member of the society's board since 2014. Blair was the President of the CFA Society of Louisiana in 2016–2017.

Blair and her husband live in New Orleans with their two young children.

A T A CONFERENCE for financial advisors several years ago, I attended a session by Tim Maurer, a well-known advisor, speaker and author who is currently the Director of Advisor Development at Buckingham Strategic Wealth. Tim began by asking the audience, "What is your first memory of money?" I wracked my brain, but in that hour, I could not determine my first money memory.

Early money memories create "money scripts," which are deeply embedded internal beliefs about money. Common money scripts include, "Hard work earns money," "Inherited wealth is bad," or "Poor people are lazy." Once developed, money scripts are difficult to change. Research on the psychology of money scripts reveals that they can fundamentally shape our lives. Understanding our money scripts can remove obstacles to achieving our financial goals in life.

The most common answer to Tim's question is the Tooth Fairy. How fascinating that an entire society has formulated its foundational beliefs about money based on a magical creature that sneaks into our bedrooms in the middle of the night to pay us for our discarded teeth. The implications are frightening if you spend too much time thinking about them.

It was not until later that evening I realized that my first money memory was the offering plate at church. The offering plate is passed around the pews to accept a weekly donation from all church members in attendance on Sunday. My first formative memory of money is of people willingly giving it away to support their church and the work it does in the community. I have often thought about how this memory shapes my financial decisions.

I pursued a career in finance because I fell in love with markets and investing during college. At first, I was a stock picker who admired Warren Buffett. Following Buffett's "buy what you know" advice, the first stock I bought was Nordstrom's department store. A few years later, I violated Buffett's suggested holding period of "forever," when I sold the stock to put down a deposit on a studio apartment in midtown Manhattan.

My investment philosophy changed when I read Charles Ellis' book *Winning the Loser's Game*. The book was given to me by my employer at the time, Michael Goodman, founder of Wealthstream Advisors, Inc. Ellis convinced me that trying to beat the market is a losing proposition. In golf, par is a good score, and avoiding bogeys is more important than making birdies. Very few professional investors beat the market consistently, after accounting for the costs. The most important takeaway from Ellis' books is that the market return is a good return. The proliferation of low-cost index funds means that the market return is ours for the taking, if only we accept it. I have not purchased an individual stock since reading that book.

I have always prioritized saving by paying myself first. Early in my career this amounted to nothing more than a small contribution to a 401(k) plan. I made sure to get the employer match by contributing the minimum amount required to earn it. Ten years ago, I relocated to New Orleans and made a decision to hang my own shingle as a financial planner and investment advisor. To fund the business and lack of salary, I spent most of the retirement savings I had accumulated during the first decade of my career. I believe this was the best investment decision I ever made. While I was terrible at prospecting and growing an advisory business, I began to promote myself through my website, blog, and social media. These efforts raised my profile as an advisor to a national level. I often joke that the money spent on my website was the most expensive job interview of my life.

In the years since, I have married, bought a starter home, and started a family. Our financial priorities include education for our three-year-old son and newborn daughter, moving to a larger family home, and somewhere in the distant future, something not quite resembling retirement. As a financial planner, I have watched many people retire. Some sail into a blissful new life filled with travel, friends, hobbies, and activities. Others struggle to find a sense of purpose. I worry I would find myself in the later camp. Retirement is a goal in the sense that we want a portfolio that could sustain our living expenses if we were no longer earning a paycheck.

By following the ethos of paying myself first, a portion of every paycheck is automatically added to my 401(k) plan, a 529 college savings account for both children, and a cash reserve account. My goal is to separate myself from these earnings and invest them towards our long-term goals. I try to keep six months of living expenses in a cash reserve, which gets dipped into throughout the year for various home repair projects and unexpected expenses.

Most years I enroll in a health insurance policy that allows me to make contributions to a Healthcare Savings Account (HSA). HSA funds can be invested in the market, allowing earnings to accrue for health-related expenses later in life. HSA savings are made with pre-tax dollars, earnings inside the account grow tax-deferred, and qualified withdrawals are tax and penalty free. This triple-tax advantage is rare. However, HSA eligible insurance policies carry high deductibles. This year, for example, I chose a plan with a lower deductible in expectation of the birth of my child. I hope to resume HSA savings in future years and build a savings account for future healthcare costs.

I invest my retirement and after-tax accounts in the same portfolios I recommend to clients. My mix of stocks and bonds is based on two things: time horizon and risk tolerance. My time horizon is long. I plan to work for at least three more decades, and my children are very young. My risk tolerance is high because I have the benefit of time and because I work in the industry and therefore intimately understand the relationship between risk and return. That does not mean my portfolio is 100% invested in stocks. Instead, I place 80% in stocks and 20% in bonds. Bonds reduce downside volatility and provide dry powder for rebalancing during bear markets.

I sit on the investment committee at my firm. We spend the majority of our time contemplating what we call "the most important decision," which is the asset allocation of our clients' portfolios. This decision includes the mix of domestic and international stocks, small and large cap companies, and exposure to factors such as value, momentum, and shareholder yield. Afterwards, we determine the mechanism for implementing the asset allocation decision. We combine both long-term strategic allocation with medium-term tactical decisions. If international stocks are cheap compared to stocks in the US, we will tilt the portfolio more towards international stocks than the benchmark suggests. My portfolio follows the same investment recommendations I make to clients. The result is a globally diversified mix of stocks and bonds invested in low-cost mutual funds and exchange-traded funds (ETFs).

The 529 plans for my children are invested in age-based mutual funds managed by Vanguard. The Louisiana 529 plan includes a generous 2% match on annual contributions from the state. This is on top of a state income tax deduction of up to $4,800 per married couple per year. As my children approach college age, the asset allocation of these investments will shift from primarily stocks to primarily cash and bonds. At the rate of college tuition increases we have seen in recent years, it could cost over $1 million to send my children to a public in-state university.

I make one exception to investing in anything outside the portfolios I recommend to clients. The investment management industry is small, and over the years I have formed relationships with some incredibly talented people whose investment recommendations are available through ETFs. One is Perth Tolle, the creator of Life + Liberty Indexes. Her methodology ranks emerging market countries based on their human and economic freedoms. The thesis is that freedom wins in a capitalist market. I purchased a small amount of her ETF in my Roth IRA. I expect I will make an additional exception or two for products from people I admire.

My experience as a financial advisor has taught me that the "why" is more important than the "how" when it comes to investing. My financial goals are much more important than the alpha or the Sharpe ratio of my portfolio. As long as I prioritize paying myself first and avoid unnecessary mistakes, I am confident that my investment portfolio will do its job.

Leighann Miko

NET WORTH ≠ SELF WORTH

Leighann Miko is a CERTIFIED FINANCIAL PLANNER™ and the founder of Equalis Financial, a Los Angeles-based independent fee-only firm providing financial planning, business management, and investment management services.

With a passion to empower and equip underserved communities, Leighann works with thoughtfully ambitious professionals, especially LGBTQ+ creatives in the entertainment industry. Her goal is to help them stay in their right brain by acting as a stand-in for their left brain.

With a commitment to human-centered financial planning, Leighann devotes time to understand the whole person before addressing their finances. This intentional approach was born from a desire to help others create the financially secure life she never thought she'd have. Having grown up in a household faced with constant financial volatility, Leighann recognizes the value of financial stability. Knowing what it's like to be underestimated herself, her mission became clear: to balance the financial playing field for all.

> *"Owning our story can be hard but not nearly as difficult as spending our lives running from it."*
>
> —Brene Brown, *The Gifts of Imperfection*

M AN, AM I tired of running! And as part of that marathon, money has never been a pleasant topic. It's been traumatizing and debilitating. Rarely has it represented something positive and when it did, it was a temporary illusion that I had created to manipulate myself. There is a thin psychological line between the truth and self-preservation. As I get older, I'm finding it more and more difficult to see that line clearly as it pertains to my past.

I grew up in a volatile financial environment. Stability, when it existed, was short-lived and only came at the hands of an emotionally volatile step-father, which was a very ill-fitting title for him. Let's just say the day he and my mom separated when I was 12 is still one of the happiest days of my life.

From that point on, my brothers and I spent most of our formative adolescent years being raised by a single mother who dropped out of high school after 10th grade. She did what she thought best to protect us from the harsh realities of being dependent on welfare and how that was perceived by our community. It was our family secret. She would only shop at grocery stores way beyond our city limits to ensure there was absolutely no chance someone we knew would see us using food stamps. Though my mom never directly explained why she refused to shop at our local store, I knew she was embarrassed and that stuck with me. Lesson learned; your value is tied to your net worth.

Despite my mom's hustle and determination to make ends meet, there were many times I would come home from school to find the power or gas had been disconnected. I'd mostly taken it upon myself to call and beg the power company to reconnect the utilities so my mom wouldn't have to handle personal business while at work. I was 13. When it wasn't the utilities or a car being repossessed, it was pleading with landlords to delay the eviction process, several times to no avail. And every time shit hit the fan, you could sense the defeat within her. Seeing the look of fear and disappointment on her face through the smile she desperately tried to slap on was my motivation to avoid repeating that cycle. And I did avoid repeating that cycle, kind of.

Skip forward to legal adulthood. I remember applying for and receiving my very first credit card. It felt like Christmas morning. I had just turned 18 and I was suckered in by the ability to pick the design of the card. (Marketers know what they are doing!) When it came in the mail several weeks later, I remember that little piece of green plastic bringing me a ridiculous amount of joy. All $200 of credit limit. Freedom.

I said to myself, "it's just for emergencies." That lasted all of two weeks. But what a cute thought.

I still remember the first purchase I made. It was a blue and green striped top from Pacific Sunware that set me back about $18. That tug of the loose psychological thread is all it took to set off a chain of events that would span an 18-year period. Not to mention the short couple of weeks it took to max out that $200 credit limit. My money issues had finally become an adult and it was time to let them be free and make their own stupid decisions.

The internal conflict around the value of money created such a divide in my psyche that it's as if I had developed two parallel personalities. There was the desperate child in me trying to fill the void by binge shopping for meaningless things to get that instant gratification. And there was the responsible, educated adult who knew the consequences of my actions and refused to ever pay full price for anything, despite being able to afford to do so. Which is still something I refuse to do to this day. Consequently, my spending habits vacillated between the urge to spend it all and the need to hoard it all. Though they spent most of the time in the former.

In 2019 I made mental health a priority so I could give myself the space to move from the person I think I am to the person I actually am. Part of that is absolute brutal honesty with myself, especially as it pertains to my motivations and values. Despite my relative success, there still exists a deep disconnect between where I am and where I think I am in life. I still feel like that kid on welfare and that's what people see me as. But on paper, I am an expert in personal finance, yet I can't wrap my educated head around my own finances in a meaningful way.

What's held me back for so long is one repeating thought. I was never supposed to make it this far. It's like I slipped through a hole in the gate and I'm just waiting for security to pull me out of line and tell me I'm not tall enough for this ride. I really thought I knew why I got into the personal finance industry. I was wrong. Thirteen years into my career it's become crystal clear. I chose this business to help people create a life I never thought I would have.

I always dreamed about what it would be like to drive a reliable car that wasn't going to be repossessed, to own a home that I couldn't be evicted from, to travel more than 30 miles from my house, to have a sense of financial security. So, I thought, at least I can help people do all of those things and then experience them second-hand. It was kind of like playing dress up. I could try on each client's lifestyle, take it for a test drive in my head and then hop back into reality.

Well, now it's out there. Now it's time for the turnaround and as personal finance guru George Kinder would ask "How do you want it to be instead?"

So, this isn't so much about how I've perfected the recipe for living my values and aligning my spending, saving, and investment decisions around that. This is all still new to me.

It's an open letter to myself and anyone else who needs a reminder that this takes work and practice. It isn't until we truly discover what is most important to us that we can take meaningful action to live into that truth. And contrary to popular belief, it's okay to make decisions that don't make sense on paper. One thing I never do or recommend anyone do is make a decision based solely on the monetary benefit or consequence. There's another side to the coin that is equally, if not more, important.

The way I've come to guide my spending is knowing that my dollars are serving not only me, but others as well. I try to spend my money in ways that have the greatest benefit to the most people. I primarily donate money to local grassroots organizations rather than the big corporate funded organizations. It's the local soldiers in the field that are really making a difference. I purchase gifts from organizations that create employment opportunities or provide job training to help break vicious cycles of homelessness and drug addiction, especially in the Los Angeles area where I've spent my entire life.

Though I battle the ease and speed of Amazon, I try desperately to shop local and support small businesses whenever possible. I rarely eat at large chain restaurants and I tip well because restaurant servers are underappreciated. Where are my former servers at?! And those who know me even a little bit, know that I love craft beer, so I spend my money at a local mom-and-pop bottle shop that stocks beer from small breweries both local and national.

As I've come to terms with my past, I know that future me will really appreciate present me not giving into instant gratification, especially when my values do not align with the purchase. That's how I have shifted my thinking regarding saving. Gaining a deeper understanding of what's really important to me has given me more control over how I spend my money, or rather don't spend it. Though asking myself "do I really value this?" before every purchase isn't practical, knowing that future me is dangling that carrot from a stick certainly helps.

Some things will never change. I will always root for the underdog. I will always support the hustle. I will always be my friends' and clients' biggest cheerleader.

Perth Tolle

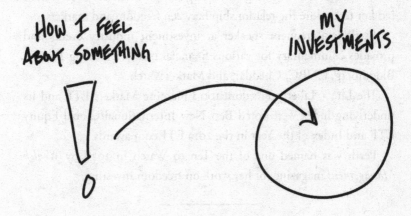

Perth Tolle

———

Perth Tolle is the founder of Life + Liberty Indexes. Prior to forming Life + Liberty Indexes, Perth was a private wealth advisor at Fidelity Investments in Los Angeles and Houston. Prior to Fidelity, Perth lived and worked in Beijing and Hong Kong, where her observations led her to explore the relationship between freedom and markets.

Perth is a frequent speaker at investment industry events and provides commentary for various financial media including *Barron's*, Bloomberg, CNBC, Cheddar, and MarketWatch.

The Life + Liberty Freedom 100 Emerging Markets ETF and its underlying index were voted Best New International/Global Equity ETF and Index of the Year in the 2019 ETF.com awards.

Perth was named one of the Ten to Watch in 2020 by *Wealth Management* magazine for her work on freedom investing.

———

L EAVE IT TO an Uber driver to drop some wisdom that helps formulate your perspective on investing. A couple years ago in Orange County, my driver, Charlie Clark, and I were chatting to pass the time. He told me that he was Gwen Stefani's voice coach when she was in high school. He knew a lot about music and the creative process. A couple things he said stuck with me:

> "An artist will create in a way that conveys how they feel about something as well as how they think about it."

and

> "Words and notes are not music, the stuff on the page is abstract, you have to turn them into life."

To illustrate, he then proceeded to belt out his own renditions of Frank Sinatra. The songs were unnecessary to prove his point as I already knew exactly what he meant. For me, investing is as much a creative pursuit and form of expression as an intellectual or scientific exercise. And I express myself through indexing. My investments are a way to convey how I feel about something, as well as how I think about it. Through my work as an indexer, my mission is to create ways for others to be able to do the same.

I see my personal investments as tools to be used in service of this mission—words and notes on a page. It's one thing to accumulate words and notes, another to put them to music, and give them life.

Before I started my index company, I was a financial advisor at Fidelity Investments. I loved this role. Yet I clearly remember a time right before I left Fidelity, when I was looking at my brokerage statements, and thinking that I had come to a point where making more money seemed meaningless and unnecessary.

I knew I was being called to start my own company to bring freedom investing to life. It was hard to leave Fidelity, because it felt like home, and starting something new, especially an ETF, was extremely risky. But I could no longer deny the fire inside, and decided it was worth the risk. My savings and investments at that time gave me enough financial security to take the leap. My goal now with my portfolio is to keep it growing at a sustainable rate so I can focus on my company's mission without worrying about personal finances.

With my own investments, I'm a combination of two clichés:

1. I'm an investment professional who tends to neglect my own accounts: For the most part, I hold the most low-maintenance instruments possible, such as ETFs and index mutual funds
2. I have skin in the game: I am extremely overweight freer emerging markets in the ETF based on my own index.

My investable assets can be divided into four goals/buckets (and the asset allocations within each).

1. Short term/emergency funds (100% money market).
I keep a couple years of living expenses and emergency funds in money markets because I'm running a new and pre-profit business from which I do not currently draw a salary. This is the slush fund that lets me keep the dream alive until my company is profitable.

2. General investing and cash for investment opportunities (50% stocks, 50% cash).

This is a brokerage account in which I hold stocks and ETFs that are not part of my core strategy. They're companies I enjoy and believe in, or ETFs with themes that I think are promising. I hold some of my fellow independent ETF issuers' products in this account. One of the things I love the most about the ETF business is getting to do it alongside brilliant people with innovative ideas, and getting to use their products before they become mainstream.

3. Retirement (90% stocks, 10% bonds).

This is the largest asset pool out of my investment goals/buckets, mostly rolled over from my Fidelity 401(k). Here I have some extremely low-cost Fidelity index funds—large, mid, and small cap US equities. At some point I intend to switch these out for corresponding ETFs, but it's not a priority currently as I do not trade them at all. I get made fun of by my ETF colleagues for still having mutual funds in my account. To people in the ETF industry, mutual funds, even index mutual funds, seem anachronistic. But at this cost, in an IRA, I'll allow it. I also have some bond funds that I have neglected to switch into lower-cost ETF counterparts.

The remainder and bulk of this account is in emerging markets equities in the form of the Freedom 100 EM ETF (Ticker: FRDM)—the ETF based on my index. This position makes up more than half of my long-term holdings across all accounts. It is a freedom-weighted emerging markets strategy that uses personal and economic freedom metrics to determine country weights and allocations. Freer countries get higher weights, less free countries get lower weights, and the worst actors are excluded. So there's no allocation to the worst rights offenders like China, Russia, and Saudi Arabia.

I believe in the long-term growth potential of emerging markets and in the power of free people to drive that growth. Since most other emerging markets funds have about 50% of their allocations in autocratic regimes due to market capitalization weighting, freedom-weighting makes much more sense to me. At the same time, it's a way for me to express my preference for freedom in my portfolio.

This is a very aggressive allocation and as I write this we are experiencing a bounce off the lows of the COVID crisis of 2020. There were several times during the last few months when I had to be talked out of taking unwise actions in my accounts by friends and colleagues with more years of experience and who could see things from a third party unemotional perspective. That's the power of accountability from people you trust and respect.

Sticking with an investment plan is hard, and I do not recommend going it alone. I am fortunate to be surrounded by investment experts who know the business I'm in. A good financial advisor that knows your story is invaluable for most investors. That said, the one thing I never considered reducing is my position in FRDM. That's a behavioral investing hack—invest in what you believe in and have strong conviction about, and you'll likely experience better outcomes just by being able to avoid selling at the worst times.

4. Charitable giving (20% stocks, 80% bonds).

I use a charitable gift account to contribute highly appreciated stocks in kind, organize distributions, and get immediate tax benefits without having to keep a receipt for each recipient. Many years ago, before I had any money, I bought one token share of GOOG because they stood up to the Chinese government regarding censorship. That share multiplied itself over time and has since been transferred into this account in kind. My most highly appreciated security currently is AAPL, and I plan to use some of those Apple shares for gifting.

One thing I would be careful about when using this type of account is the temptation to delay distributions to keep investing in the giving account, which defeats its purpose. The organizational and in kind contribution features are nice, but remember the goal is to get contributions to recipients for their real world use. Due to the short time frame during which contributions into this account turn into distributions out of it, I use a conservative (20/80) allocation for these funds.

These are my personal investments only. I have not discussed business assets which include my own capital contributions as well as those of my limited partners, and which I consider a private investment.

I really believe that if you're called to do something, you will be equipped for it, and sometimes, you'll even get little affirmations along the way. My encounter with Charlie was one of those. It left me with the realization that investing can be a form of expression. And I was reminded that I am here to make music, not to accumulate notes on a page, but to turn them into life.

Joshua Rogers

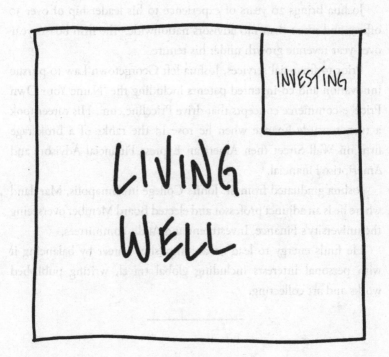

Joshua D. Rogers is the founder and CEO of Arete Wealth, a firm specializing in wealth management for high-net worth individuals and institutions.

Joshua brings 20 years of experience to his leadership of over 30 offices and more than 140 advisors nationwide. The firm boasts year-over-year revenue growth under his tenure.

Prior to financial services, Joshua left Georgetown Law to pursue innovation and co-invented patents including the 'Name Your Own Price' e-commerce concepts that drive Priceline.com. His career took a turn towards finance when he rose in the ranks of a brokerage firm on Wall Street then American Express Financial Advisors and Ameriprise Financial.

Joshua graduated from St. John's College in Annapolis, Maryland where he is an adjunct professor and elected Board Member overseeing the university's Finance, Investment and Audit committees.

He finds energy to lead an accomplished career by balancing it with personal interests including global travel, writing published works and art collecting.

Aphorisms on investing in the style of Nietzsche and La Rochefoucauld

THE WRITING STYLE of the aphorism is dangerous in that it tempts the reader to think they are reading something of a more minor literary or philosophical genre. We are tempted to think of the maxim or aphorism as simply a playful recreation, the random musings of a less serious mind than the more continuous and systematic narrative that serious science demands.

Yet I have found that the most penetrating and serious philosophical insights I still remember 20 years later have very often come from thinkers who chose the aphoristic style—starting with Heraclitus, to La Rochefoucauld, Nietzsche, and now in today's world... Twitter! Much wisdom today is forced to be condensed into Twitter-sized... aphorisms!

In my view the aphorism is the style of the humble thinker. Instead of lecturing to the reader with long paragraphs and run-on sentences, the aphorism seeks not to explain or dictate, but rather to describe one's own experience in bite-sized chunks.

The aphorism doesn't take itself too seriously. The writer of the aphorism only knows what Socrates said was all he knew... that he does not know anything!

One can therefore take my aphorisms or leave them, for these are just my musings on investing, and more importantly, living well.

Where to invest

- Public markets have become so efficient because of the advancements in information technology that it is impossible to achieve any informational advantage (legally). Therefore, I am more interested in investing in markets that are less efficient and where information advantages can be easily and legally gained. Examples of these types of markets are: real estate (all sub-asset classes), privately held operating businesses, venture capital, fine art, fine wine and spirits, watches, collectible automobiles, antiques, antiquities, rare earth metals, and cryptocurrencies.

- Warren Buffett famously said, "invest in what you know." I take it one step further and assert "invest in things you love to own and that you are obsessed with researching and gaining knowledge about."

- I have a strong preference for investing in tangible hard assets—even better if I can also get some sort of use or enjoyment in my life from the assets.

- Looking at my own balance sheet, my largest asset and biggest single investment is my own business. I have always felt that I would much rather invest in something that I control as opposed to something that I have no control over, like the S&P 500 index. I would rather be the driver of the car as opposed to a passenger on board a bus along with millions of other people in the back just praying the bus doesn't crash.

- I prefer the idea that if I lose money by investing in my own business, I have no one to blame but myself. But when one invests in public stocks, you can blame all kinds of other people or factors outside of your control if things do not go well. This is a path that leads to a victim mentality about life and circumstances. Reject such a path.

- After you invest in yourself—aka your own business, or businesses, that you have some measure of control in, e.g. a voting Board seat—invest in real estate. In my experience real estate is the second most reliable way to build wealth over the very long term.

- I personally own outright, or am a limited partner in, a wide range of real estate sub-asset classes. My investments include: single family residential, multi-family residential, farm land, industrial distribution centers, and self-storage. I have made exceptional returns (particularly tax adjusted) in almost all of my real estate investments.

- Invest in assets you love. In my case I love visual art. Art history has always fascinated me and I love studying it. Living with great art beautifies and enhances your life immeasurably. Plus, art is a highly inefficient market where major information advantages can be had. Art consistently holds its value over time and in all economic conditions. Art is one of the few asset classes other than angel investing and venture capital where it is common to achieve returns north of 1000%. Yet with such enormous upside potential, art is also remarkably stable. Since 1985 the whole contemporary art market (auction level) has returned 7.5% per year.

- I also love fine automobiles and fine wines and spirits. Not only can you make great returns, but you also get enjoyment from your investments! Can you say the same thing about owning a stock in a company or an ETF? You can't hang an ETF on your wall, or drink it, or drive it!

- Always look to the future and take a few chances by investing in futuristic companies or new asset classes. In my case, my bias in favor of hard assets combined with my experience during Internet 1.0 as a co-inventor of Priceline.com, led me to begin investing in Bitcoin and other cryptocurrencies three years ago. I have since also started a cryptocurrency hedge fund with two other partners who are veterans in the blockchain/crypto space and are members of the Satoshi Roundtable. Bitcoin has been the single best performing asset of the past decade by a mile.

The law of giving

- People who are overly obsessed with their personal investments (e.g., watching their portfolio 10–20 times per day or similar) may achieve decent results in the short or medium term, but long term they tend to self-destruct (their portfolios/net worth that is) by being too close to it, too emotional, and too tight-fisted about their money. I have grown my net worth by adhering to a principle in Deepak Chopra's 1994 book, *The Seven Spiritual Laws of Success.* The 2nd Law is the Law of Giving. Each day bring whoever you encounter a gift: a compliment, positive energy, a flower. Gratefully receive gifts. Keep wealth circulating by giving and receiving care, value, information, appreciation, and love.

- Money and the accumulation of wealth works like the circulation of blood within the body. If a person is always worried about their money, afraid of risk and loss, tight-fisted, not charitable, suspicious, obsessed about fees, etc., it is akin to tying a tourniquet on a limb of the body—you cut off the proper circulation and flow of blood which leads to amputation or death. Instead, keep the money moving! Be generous, take risks with your investments (you will be rewarded), let other people make money too, invest in people who you like and trust. This kind of approach creates an energy of giving and positivity which results in more circulation, more abundance, and thus abundant investment returns (but also spiritual returns).

- Karma *may* be important in achieving wealth accumulation, but karma is *definitely* important in wealth preservation.

On taxes

- The US tax code immensely favors two types of investments: owning your own business, and direct real estate investing/ ownership (not REITs or some other publicly available security that invests in real estate). Just as traders say "Don't fight the Fed," I say, "Don't fight the IRS, go with their flow and let the money flow to me!"
- Worry less about the fees involved in investing and more about the taxes. Taxes create a drag on your investment of somewhere between 20%–35%. Fees will never exceed 5% even at their most egregious.

On marriage and divorce

- One of the best investments you can make is paying for a solid pre-nup before getting married. Divorce (with kids involved) is crazy expensive and thus a very, very bad investment.

On financial advisors

- Having been a registered financial advisor professionally for over 20 years, it is an acknowledged fact in the trade that at least 75% of professional financial advisors are cobblers whose children have no shoes.
- Wall Street is the only place where people driving a Toyota Camry advise people with Bentleys on how to manage their money.
- I think it's natural that the longer any craftsman works in his trade, the less likely he is to enjoy or consume the thing he makes or deals with—hence the baker who does not like to eat bread, and the butcher who goes vegetarian. In my case, after so many years of analyzing stocks and public markets, I now find investing in stocks, bonds, mutual funds, and ETFs boring and joyless.

- I have yet to meet any person whose primary focus in investing is minimizing fees, who is also a happy, well-adjusted, enjoyable person to be around.
- Everyone should have a financial advisor if for no other reason than to have a sounding board who is less emotional about your money than you are.

On the proper mentality in investing

- In my experience, the more intensely and emotionally a lot of people "hate on" a particular investment, that is a good signal to buy. This is exactly what has happened to me with Bitcoin over the past three years (meanwhile my returns have been approximately 500% over that period), and what happened to me with buying multi-family real estate in early 2009.
- Avoid the loss avoidance tendency. When facing a loss in an investment, ask yourself what opportunity cost are you giving up by holding onto the losing investment hoping it will come back? Good traders move on quickly and unemotionally from losing investments to get refocused on good investments. Not to mention I have found that holding onto losing investments (or allowing yourself to excessively focus on the losers) drags down your whole mental state, which is harmful in a variety of ways. This goes back to one of my earlier principles of investing, which is to maintain a loose mental grip on your investments. Have humor. Relax. Smile a lot. Recognize that all investing involves risk and therefore means you will lose sometimes.
- I had a rich older cousin who after retiring to a huge house on the beach in the Hamptons told me over cigars and whiskey, "I started 10 businesses in my life. The only reason why I am rich is because six of them succeeded and four of them were total failures. Which means it was a swing of just one venture that made all the difference."
- He who cares least, wins.

Jenny Harrington

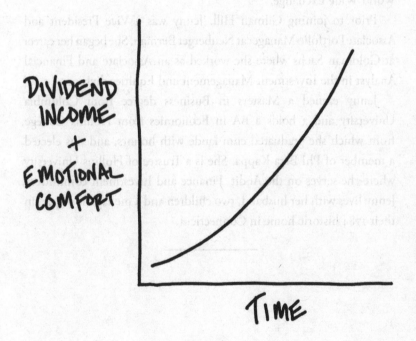

Jenny Harrington is the CEO of Gilman Hill Asset Management, and Portfolio Manager of the firm's flagship Equity Income strategy. She is also a contributor to CNBC, appearing on the Halftime Report and World Wide Exchange.

Prior to joining Gilman Hill, Jenny was a Vice President and Associate Portfolio Manager at Neuberger Berman. She began her career at Goldman Sachs where she worked as an Associate and Financial Analyst in the Investment Management and Equities divisions.

Jenny earned a Masters in Business degree from Columbia University and a holds a BA in Economics from Hollins College, from which she graduated cum laude with honors, and was elected a member of Phi Beta Kappa. She is a Trustee of Hollins University where she serves on the Audit, Finance and Investment committees. Jenny lives with her husband, two children and a menagerie of pets in their 1784 historic home in Connecticut.

I AM A dividend income investor—personally and professionally. What I buy for my clients, I buy for myself.

Okay, okay, I may have a rogue position in Facebook that I bought in 2012 after it traded below the IPO price… and maybe a few shares of Twitter that I bought after I heard Bill Miller make an incredibly compelling case in 2015. But that's it for me and the growth stocks.

In my personal portfolios, I own only publicly traded stocks, and high dividend payers at that, which is not what most people expect from a 44-year-old extrovert. No funds of any sort, no alternatives, no bonds, just stocks. I don't even own shares in my brother's hugely successful ice cream company, because I refuse to risk my personal relationship with him over money.

Instead, I buy MLPs for their consistent income and tax-favorability. I love the real estate investment trusts that collect rent and pay it out to shareholders. I love knowing that each company that I invest in will pay me cash each quarter and that all of my return is not dependent entirely on other investors' often-fickle perception of the "correct" valuation for a company.

I had a wonderful client, Betty, who taught me an important lesson. I was in my early 30s, Betty was 92. I was fresh out of Columbia Business School and filled with idealism. As I took over management of Betty's all-stock portfolio, I prudently suggested that she add bonds to her portfolio. She essentially said to me, "I've owned stocks since I was a kid when my father bought them for me, then my husband

and I bought stocks, and since he died (decades earlier) I have bought stocks for myself. They have always provided me all the income that I need to live on. Bonds don't grow and neither does their income. Why would I ever want to own anything but stocks?" Because of my personal long-term horizon and because I value income, I have since been firmly entrenched in the Betty school of asset allocation.

I became a champion of dividends largely by accident. In 2001, I had a client call and say, "Hey Jen, I'm getting ready to retire, so I'll need income. But I'm only 55 and will need growth, too. What can you do for me?" To achieve these not-always-compatible objectives, there really was only one viable approach. So, I repositioned his core US stock portfolio into a dividend income portfolio with the objective of generating a 5% or better dividend yield, with the potential for additional capital appreciation over the long term. Thus began my deep love of dividend income investing.

What I soon came to believe was that dividends are the purest mechanism for shareholder return. Cash comes in to a company, and a good corporate steward executing on a solid business plan can return a portion of that cash flow directly to its investors. It is simple to understand, but not always easy to identify which companies will be able to execute successfully.

Philosophically, having been indoctrinated by the value leanings of my former employer, Neuberger Berman, and by graduate studies with Bruce Greenwald at Columbia Business School, it is perhaps not surprising that a value undercurrent runs through me, and dividend investing intersects nicely with that mindset. It simply makes sense to me that the best long-term investments are likely to be found among companies that are trading at a discount to their realistic value. Such discounts represent both opportunity and a margin of safety. In the case of dividend stocks, a realistic value can be determined by a combination of evaluating the net-present-value of future cash flows, and by considering other factors like future earnings growth and catalysts for multiple expansion.

Most people, if they think of income investing at all, probably picture elderly retirees collecting their dividend payments from boring companies. And they wouldn't be entirely wrong. The majority of the companies in which I invest are mature businesses with long histories of consistent cash-flow generation through a variety of economic cycles. This would include companies like AT&T, IBM and Verizon, all of which have paid dividends for over 35 years. Clearly, this is not the stuff of riveting cocktail party conversations, at least not at any point after 1985. And yet, from an intellectual and an emotional perspective, investing in dividend-paying stocks perfectly resonates for me.

As a true-believer in dividend investing, I will point out that it is a much more dynamic and less monolithic niche than one might expect. Indeed, some of my best investments have been in companies that would not have been thought of as traditional "dividend stocks." Take Western Digital, a maker of data storage, for example. The pricing of Western Digital's products is highly cyclical, and the share price tends to follow suit. However, by taking a slightly longer-term perspective, one can see that over three or five years, the cash flows were consistent, and well able to support the dividend that the company initiated in 2012. Because of the movement in the share price, we were able to purchase Western Digital for about $40.00 per share, with a $2.00 dividend in early 2017. We sold it about a year later for $102.

Another one of my favorite investments was in Douglas Dynamics, a manufacturer of snowplow blades with superb operational and management capabilities. In researching Douglas, we were able to see that on a year-by-year basis, the sales of snowplow blades is lumpy, but over eight-year cycles, the sales are astonishingly consistent. Douglas' leadership team managed the company, as well as its dividend policy, to this eight-year cycle. In the late summer of 2011, as US debt was downgraded, we were able to invest in this wonderful company and held the shares for seven years, enjoying significant capital appreciation as the strength of the business slowly became recognized and appreciated by the broader market. At the same time, we were able to collect consistent income throughout the many ups and downs that the market experience over that period.

I grew up in a financially volatile household and witnessed the downside of counting on possible big wins as justification for living above the means. The current income provided by investing in dividend stocks simply provides me with a level of emotional comfort. Knowing that income will flow into my portfolios through thick and thin (as it has through the financial crisis of 2008/09, the US debt downgrade of 2011, the taper tantrum of 2013, the oil price plunge of 2015/16, the flash bear market of 2018, and now the coronavirus crisis) brings me comfort, conviction and confidence. As we all know, in times of trouble, cash becomes king.

I do also invest heavily in myself and my business. I have had the same babysitter for my kids since the day my daughter was born in 2007—back then, I was just starting up at Gilman Hill and had to subsidize the expense with proceeds from my retirement account, but I knew that having the flexibility of that kind of childcare was the only way I could fully focus on my career and considered it a major investment in my family's future. Thankfully, that one has paid off.

I invest significantly in Gilman Hill where we have superb (and expensive!) systems, serene and functional office space, and an extremely high quality, meticulously selected staff. I fully believe that you get what you pay for and I am happy to pay fairly, hopefully even generously, to be able to hire the best people. They allow Gilman Hill to thrive and this allows me to do my job and live my life with the confidence and relief of knowing that I have a true team of wonderful people alongside me.

Michael Underhill

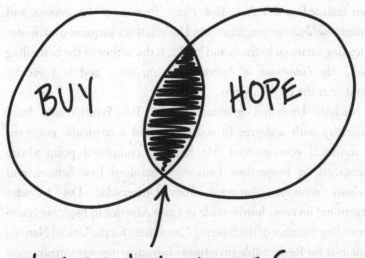

BUY HOPE

NOT AN INVESTMENT STRATEGY

Michael Underhill is Founder & CIO of Capital Innovations. He has pioneered several unconventional portfolio strategies that are now widely applied: global listed infrastructure, listed timber, listed agribusiness, and multi-asset real return. The products have been featured in *The New York Times*, *Pensions & Investments*, and *Institutional Investor* magazine. Mr. Underhill is a frequent contributor to leading financial journals and books, is the author of the bestselling book, *The Handbook of Infrastructure Investing*, and is a Faculty Member at the CFA Institute.

Michael Underhill graduated from The Pennsylvania State University with a degree in economics and a curricular emphasis in statistical econometrics. He has also completed postgraduate coursework at Pepperdine University, Stanford Law School, and graduate economic program from Universidad Del Salvador (Argentina) on cross-border trade in Latin America in 1998. He is also a founding member of the Steering Committee for the United Nations' Principles for Responsible Investment Infrastructure workstream, and founder of the Underhill Cancer Research Foundation.

I GREW UP south of Pittsburgh, Pennsylvania, the youngest of five kids spanning 14 years. My father, Edward Underhill, was born in an impoverished Polish neighborhood called Lawrenceville. I was raised listening to his stories of overcoming fierce odds and soldiering on; including recollections about how his family lost everything in the Great St. Patrick's Day Flood of 1936 when flood levels peaked at 46 feet.

My father was a World War II USMC veteran from the Pacific theater of war, seeing combat in Tinian, Saipan and the bloody battle of Tarawa. Needless to say, our family dinner table discussion was infused with military rhetoric, expletives and how people were always starving in Africa so everyone in the family needed to be a producing asset—generating cash flow for the family—not a liability. I learned early on that there was incalculable value in hard work, grit and being self-sufficient by living on your cash flow.

My first job at age eight was answering phones at our family real estate business on Sunday mornings. We had a "second phone line" that rang in our kitchen, so no opportunity was missed to connect with a potential customer. At age 10, I was reassigned to framing houses as an unskilled carpenter as my math skills were exceedingly better than my customer service skills.

By age 12, I started a landscaping business and recruited my friend, Sammy Rockwell, as a partner. Being the budding adolescents that we were, we named the business "S&M Lawn Service." The sign on the truck was interesting and housewives just stared shockingly as we pulled the truck into the neighborhood. By age 16, I bought a Scottsdale long bed pickup truck, additional landscaping equipment and secured our first commercial contract with a Thorn Run subdivision. Managing a business in my teen years taught me invaluable lessons in capital allocation and cash flow: P/L, accounting, marketing, finance, managing payroll, equipment maintenance, scheduling, and logistics all were tangible aspects of daily life, not just some abstract business terms in a textbook. It was all about cash flow.

My college years were spent pursuing a quantitative economics degree and completing the internship program at Lehman Brothers. During my time at Lehman, the company had undergone a merger with American Express to focus on brokerage business. I spent the better part of three years creating and implementing a strategic asset allocation software program to help brokers better manage their retail clients' portfolios while splitting my time conducting municipal bond analysis. This was a bit of a strange balancing act, but it beat cutting grass or any other manual labor. The lessons were immeasurable: trying to gauge risk and return, tax-exempt income sources, taxable equivalent yield calculations, and of course cash flow.

The old saying at Lehman was investing is predicated on two tenets:

1. The performance of individual securities is unpredictable, period.
2. The performance of portfolios of securities is unpredictable on any short-term basis; what is predictable is cash flow.

After Lehman, I was fortunate to work for some of the largest asset management firms in the world (Federated, Janus, Invesco, AllianceBernstein). In 2007, I started my own firm—Capital Innovations LLC. Capital Innovations is focused on real asset investing through dual lenses of public markets as well as private markets.

Inflation may not be everyone's concern, but when I look at the period of 1900–2019, inflation has clocked in at 3% per annum.

Doesn't sounds like much? Inflation of 2% a year for 30 years reduces your purchasing power by 45%. Inflation therefore brings "longevity risk" into play for all investors—this being the likelihood that one will outlive one's financial resources, or that a retiree will outlive their funds.

Numerous factors determine how different asset classes will perform, but two of the most fundamental drivers are the pace at which the economy is growing or shrinking, and whether the economy is experiencing inflation or deflation. The foundation of the institutional asset allocation framework considers expectations for both factors, then determines how to allocate assets to four primary categories, each of which serves a different purpose in an investor's portfolio.

- **Fixed income:** Preserves capital, limits volatility, provides liquidity, and hedges against unexpected deflation.
- **Absolute return:** Generates uncorrelated returns less dependent on the direction of equity and fixed income markets.
- **Equities:** Offers long-term capital appreciation.
- **Real assets**: Hedges against unexpected inflation and produces long-term total return.

Sounds simple, but present-day investors continue to dissect far-reaching policy implications of COVID-19 government actions in 2020, which include fiscal policy and global monetary policy adding yet another round of stimulus to markets in an effort to rescue the US economy. Asset allocators are faced with recalibrating allocation models to incorporate increased volatility, uncertainty, complexity, and ambiguity.

- **Volatility**—currencies, global equities, and fixed income market volatility as well as the absence of stable and predictable markets and regulation.

- **Uncertainty**—wide swings in monetary and fiscal policy over the course of months or even weeks.
- **Complexity**—markets become riskier the larger that the ETF space becomes. The shift towards passive funds has the potential to concentrate investments in a few large products which increases systemic risk, making markets more susceptible to the flows of a few large passive products. Corrections have become more extreme.
- **Ambiguity**—Investors hesitate to diversify and explore products that they are not familiar with, thus limiting their diversification.

A look at inflation figures over the last two decades reveals concerning trends.* In summary:

- The greater (lower) the degree of government involvement in the provision of a good or service the greater (lower) the price increases (decreases) over time, e.g., hospital and medical costs, college tuition, childcare with both large degrees of government funding/regulation and large price increases vs. software, electronics, toys, cars and clothing with both relatively less government funding/regulation and falling prices.
- Prices for manufactured goods (cars, clothing, appliances, furniture, electronic goods, toys) have experienced large price declines over time relative to overall inflation, wages, and prices for services (education, medical care, and childcare).
- The greater the degree of international competition for tradeable goods, the greater the decline in prices over time, e.g., toys, clothing, TVs, appliances, furniture, footwear, etc.

Institutional investors are advised to have an exposure to a mix of sectors with low correlation to each other to help reduce risk, lower volatility, and increase diversification in an investment portfolio over multiple market cycles. These benefits can help a portfolio weather

---

* Data from M. Perry, "Chart of the day... or century?", AEI.org.

market ups and downs and ensure its sector allocations do not move in lockstep when market conditions change.

My approach personally and professionally over the years has been to incorporate a healthy allocation to real assets (infrastructure, natural resources and real estate) in the range of 10%–20% of an overall portfolio. The goal is to deliver income (cash flow), capital appreciation as a driver of long-term total return and inflation protection.

Inflation will make a comeback in this cycle. Aggressive, coordinated expansion of monetary and fiscal policy will be reflationary. We see a high risk that policymakers will prolong this response disrupting the structural disinflationary forces (tech, trade and titans) of the last 30 years. Inflationary pressures will emerge with a vengeance, so be prepared.

Hope is not a strategy, denial is not a river and cash flow is always king.

Dan Egan

THE VALUE OF MONEY

Dan Egan is the Managing Director of Behavioral Finance and Investing at Betterment. He has spent his career using behavioral finance to help people make better financial and investment decisions. Dan is a published author of multiple publications related to behavioral economics. He lectures at New York University, London Business School, and the London School of Economics on the topic.

H ow I invest for myself is either incredibly boring, or very
challenging, depending on your perspective. But it starts with
the idea that money is always a servant, never a master.

Why even save at all?

I'm going to start more from a financial planning point of view. I
save because there are things (generally expenses) in the future I want
to be able to afford. I want to know and care about what I'm saving
for. Generally speaking, I want to be saving to afford these, plus a bit
more to deal with the unexpected. I then have assets I'll use to offset
those expenses.

Here's the top-level view.

What	Percent	Ex-HC percent	Percent stocks
Human capital	75%	—	—
Retirement	11%	47%	90%
House	6%	26%	—
Natural land	3%	11%	—
Emergency fund	2%	8%	30%
Daughter college fund	2%	6%	—
Previous mistakes	1%	2%	100%

149

Let's dive into each item.

Human capital

I'm about 40, and plan on working for another 20 years. So, my biggest asset is still my earning power—my ability to turn my time and effort into money. Since I began working at 16, my hourly wage has grown nearly 10-fold. That reflects a pretty steady stream of reinvesting in myself.

After college I worked and saved for two years to be able to afford a masters program with no debt. I've learned multiple programming languages, even a mobile app language. I've taken classes in graphic design, user research, databases and version control.

I've also put effort into soft skills: coaching and feedback on being a better communicator and presenter, and media training. I occasionally write essays that I want to be effective, and I hire a professional editor. Their feedback didn't solely improve the pieces they've edited—it's improved my writing substantially.

As the set and level of skills has grown, I've been able to deliver substantially more within my own company, and outside it. You'll never see anything I've designed in production, but it's been key for making the problem clear and clearing an initial path to solutions.

Finally I put effort into networking with people who are adjacent to me. While I love other behavioral finance practitioners, I'm probably not going to learn as much from them as I will from somebody who comes from a slightly different field where we can both cross pollinate. That means taking the time to reach out and converse with people who aren't directly in your own wheelhouse.

So, my biggest asset right now is me, my time and effort, and how I spend it. That's where I invest most of my attention.

Retirement

My wife and I have a joint retirement plan, aiming to retire at about 62, which is probably too early if we're honest. We both enjoy working at white collar creative jobs, and neither of us play golf, so it's hard to imagine us changing dramatically at 62. The target is set a bit early to be conservative: if we *have* to retire that early, we'll have planned for it sufficiently well. Many people retire earlier than expected, and with lower retirement balances than expected for a variety of reasons.

We both have traditional 401(k)s, Roth IRAs, and some taxable accounts. The allocation is set to 90% stocks since we have so long till retirement. I like having that slice of bonds in my portfolio when the market goes down, and I don't think I'm going to miss the upside too much in the long run.

Since we have multiple tax account types in our retirement goal, we can strategically place different asset classes into different accounts to maximize the amount of money we're going to have in retirement. This is called asset location, and just makes use of the fact that different investments have different levels of tax drag and different account types. So looking at the overall allocation, it looks perfect. But inside each account is an allocation tailored to reduce tax drag.

I'll discuss the portfolio in detail below.

House

Ah, housing... We currently have about 30% of our wealth as principal in our house. We have a 30-year fixed mortgage and are paying it down slowly. We'll always need to live somewhere, and maybe when we're in our final decades we'll do a reverse mortgage or something. But we aren't going to value our house like a liquid asset. We talk about "renting from the bank" as being a bit more tax efficient than renting, but really I just want to be able to do what I want inside my four walls.

If I don't make any positive return on my house I'll be fine with it.

Natural land

I grew up spending summers at a camp on the Chesapeake, sleeping in a tent. We live in New York City now and we want to have more exposure to nature. I don't want my daughter growing up being scared of bugs and wild animals because they are foreign to her.

To that end we're purchasing about 10 acres of land in upstate New York. This is a *very* different experience to buying a house. The land itself costs about the downpayment on what a house would. There aren't as many inspections or overhead. There is no mortgage to pay, no mortgage underwriter. We just saved up and bought the land itself.

We will camp on it, sometimes sleeping in hammocks sometimes in tents, sometimes in a utility shed when necessary. It's more glamping than roughing it, but it's definitely not a full blown residence. We are cleaning it and grooming it, making changes that make it much more pleasant like outdoor showers and kitchens, small sleeping structures, a communal dining area, etc.

I don't plan on making much of a monetary return on it. But I will be perfectly happy if 10 years from now we take memories from families and friends, a place to relax, familiarity and a comfort and familiarity with nature.

Emergency fund

One of the earliest things I did was build up a serious emergency fund. I don't want to have to take a bad replacement job under pressure, or have a medical expense ruin my family. There are a menagerie of random misfortunes that might hit you, and I wanted a big buffer to sail through it.

The emergency fund is about 80% bonds, and 20% stocks. I don't particularly need the comfort of cash compared to the long-run chance of matching inflation. If we end up never needing it, I'd had to have given up decades of inflation erosion for a very minor amount of comfort.

Charity

That's right, charity. But bear with me, this is really about tax.

Part of our financial plan is that we give away about 10% of our income every year. We don't do that with cash however, we do it (mostly) by donating stock that has large embedded taxable gains.

Since Betterment does automated tax loss harvesting for me, I usually have shares where the cost basis has been reset lower over time. If I sold these shares, I'd owe capital gains taxes on them. By donating them, I get both a tax deduction and avoid the capital gains tax.

So I maintain a goal for charitable deductions that has a high stock allocation. When I make a charitable donation, Betterment pulls the most highly appreciated shares from any taxable account, and I maximize my impact while minimizing my taxes.

The investment portfolio

So, here's the boring part. Pretty much all my money is held at Betterment. They invest me in a low-cost globally diversified portfolio of ETFs. Betterment is responsible for pretty much everything: fund due diligence, rebalancing, managing inflows and outflows, tax loss harvesting, managing the glide path, and asset location. I don't have to do much besides save and withdraw when needed.

The funds tend to be a split between Vanguard and iShares. I don't pay a ton of attention to which, because I know the process used to select them is pretty robust.

And, to be complete, hidden off to the side is a Schrödinger's investment: my options in my company. I plan to value them at $0 until proven otherwise. If I'm lucky, I'll have a lovely problem to handle—having more money than I expected to deal with. I'm not really sure what I'd do with it to be honest. If it doesn't show up, that's absolutely fine too.

Freedom from your investments

I've worked in wealth management for (to me) a long time now. Through many interactions with clients I've noticed something.

Sometimes people become owned by their money and possessions: they spend their lives managing them and taking care of them. Instead of money freeing them from concerns or anxieties, they've architected and decorated their own prison in their wealth and they can't escape for fear of losing it.

A large part of my approach to money is in reaction to this: your money is a wonderful servant and a terrible master. You should only care as much about money as what joy it can bring or pain it can remove. Otherwise, give it as little attention as possible.

Howard Lindzon

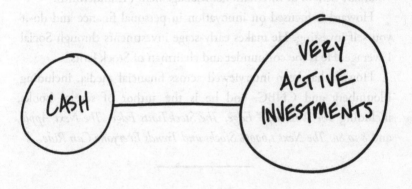

Howard Lindzon was born in Toronto and resides in Phoenix, AZ. He is married, with two children. He is a graduate of the University of Western Ontario, Arizona State University, and the American Graduate School of International Management (Thunderbird).

Howard is focused on innovation in personal finance and do-it-yourself investing. He makes early-stage investments through Social Leverage. He is the co-founder and chairman of StockTwits.

Howard has been interviewed across financial media, including Bloomberg and CNBC, and he is the author of several books, including *The Wallstrip™ Edge*, *The StockTwits Edge*, *The Next Apple*, and *8 to 80: The Next 1,000% Stocks and Trends Everyone Can Ride*.

I TAKE A lot of risk in my day job as a venture capitalist. My firm is called Social Leverage and my partners and I invest in seed stage software companies. My focus is on financial technology startups. Seed stage investments of mine whose products and brands you might have heard of include Robinhood, eToro, Ycharts, Koyfin, and Rally Rd.

I am also the co-founder of StockTwits, so it will not surprise you that I love individual stocks and not index investing.

I do not believe there is such a thing as passive investing. If you allocate even monthly to index funds you are an active investor. You have just turned over the active investing part to Vanguard or Blackrock, etc.

Most of my liquid net worth is dedicated to my investing in our Social Leverage funds. I also have made investments in other venture capital funds.

My wife and I own real estate as well, which are our largest investments outside of Social Leverage.

I also have a partnership with Charlie Bilello in a financial advisory firm called Compound Capital Advisors. Charlie is my financial advisor when it comes to market asset allocation. We talk as business partners at least once a week about the markets and about allocations once a month.

Charlie uses low cost ETFs (Vanguard, Schwab) for building client portfolios and TD Ameritrade for custody. Charlie has been writing about these trends in asset management and also building portfolios for years. After working with a client to understand their risk profile and needs, Charlie builds simple, low-cost portfolios. Charlie has also built more tactical portfolios.

Every person has a unique risk profile and needs around timing. My daughter just graduated from college and has a job starting right away. My son does not go to college but works. Right now, Ellen and I are empty nesters and Ellen has recently begun a new career in real estate. We don't have any cash flow concerns and can be very aggressive with our investments.

One reason I now do less public market investing is I have built up a tremendous amount of domain experience in financial services. It is hard to be a generalist long term (at least in my opinion) and that ties to our unique network. A bull market will bail out generalists, but recessions, bear markets and illiquidity happen. Having the domain experience to help founders and their teams survive and thrive through a bear market is an edge. If we don't need this edge… wonderful.

The other reason I do less public market investing is my unique and abundant flow of deals in the private markets. Having started Wallstrip and StockTwits, and invested at the seed stage in Robinhood and eToro, I have a point of view of course, but I also have flow. Fintech founders track me down. I obviously put that vibe out there on my blog. I am easy to find on StockTwits and Twitter, and every day on my blog I share what we are looking for. Knowing what we are looking for is part of that edge that helps me write everyday and live just enough in the future to make a difference.

My partner Gary has built four enterprise businesses, one which went public and his latest acquired by Salesforce, where he worked for four years. Gary knows modern enterprise software and how to grow teams and position products.

Between our homes, Social Leverage, my other venture investments and Charlie at Compound, that covers about 90% of our net worth.

Because of the high risk and illiquid nature of my career as a venture capitalist, I tend to keep a high cash position with my remaining liquid net worth. I have zero allocation to bonds. I don't believe bonds make sense in a zero interest rate world... at least for me.

Finally we get to my stock picking and allocations. I am very aggressive with my stock picking.

My portfolio has a high beta which at this moment (May 2020) is almost all digital, cloud-based stocks. My current mix of 50% stocks and 50% cash still allows me enough beta to feel like I can beat the S&P. I also have cash available to put to work in stocks for when the $VIX rises above 30, which in 2020 seems to be always!

I select stocks based on a few criteria. The companies have to be growing very fast and the stock prices are generally at or near all-time highs. In May 2020, that happens to be mostly NASDAQ stocks.

I also have core positions that I have held for years and hope to hold for many more years. I call them 8 to 80 stocks. They are stocks whose companies have products that 8-year-olds and 80-year-olds can't live without. Currently on this list and in my portfolio are: Zoom, Amazon, Bitcoin, Netflix, Nike, Tencent, Shopify, Google, Apple, Mastercard, McDonald's, and Facebook.

It is easy to follow along with me as I share my portfolio in real time on my StockTwits feed and my personal blog (howardlindzon.com).

Ryan Krueger

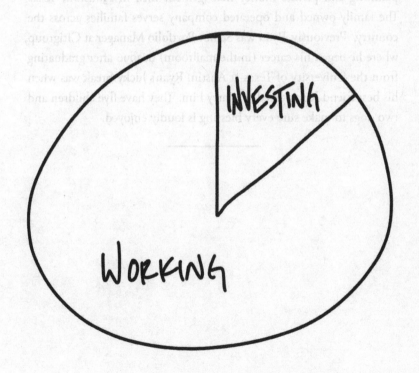

Ryan Krueger is CEO and Co-Founder of Krueger & Catalano Capital Partners. K&C was launched in 2006 as an independent investment planning and private money management firm in Houston, Texas. The family-owned and operated company serves families across the country. Previously, Ryan was Senior Portfolio Manager at Citigroup, where he began his career (in the mailroom) in 1996 after graduating from the University of Texas at Austin. Ryan's lucky break was when his best friend Kim agreed to marry him. They have five children and two dogs to make sure every blessing is loudly enjoyed.

M Y RELATIONSHIP WITH the stock market is unusual. Since I was 13 years old and asked my dad to buy 10 shares of a stock that I wanted to select, I have been invested.

When I rewind the tape to see why I was always so curious about stocks, it absolutely was not an "aha moment" or early big win. Maybe that was my lucky break. Because for some strange reason, I enjoy the ongoing challenge of questions more than any answer.

I am now certain the most important ingredient, for whatever ridiculous research process I had in mind as a kid, was added three months before. I had to beg my parents to let me get my first summer job, in order to earn those first few dollars. Their most valuable investment lesson was letting me work for every dollar invested. Not errands or allowance—I worked real jobs every summer from that point on.

Thirty-five years later, I wonder if the greatest trick the devil ever played on investors is making them think it is the investing part that matters most. The working part moves the needle more, both for the math of deposits but also in the discipline of a purpose.

In my mind, investing was never about putting something somewhere, and hoping for the best. The idea that anybody could work really hard for some extra savings, then employ those dollars into different businesses to work around the clock for them was, and still is, endlessly fascinating to me!

Mailbox money

Now that I run an investment management and financial planning firm, I still love being in charge of the research, carefully doing the math and asking more questions. Problems are easy to fix when you have only yourself to blame and use strict sell disciplines.

It never feels like making an investment to me, but always questioning an operating system to adjust. Being certain that I do not know what will happen next is what makes me excited to keep coming back. I was always curious, but what built an investment business was adding the rest of our guiding principle: Always be curious and never convinced.

The challenge is measuring companies in a way to eliminate most. It must be a repeatable process, constantly asking the data more questions. My benchmark would be simple—the selection process and discipline had to be good enough to put 100% of my own stock market exposure in the portfolio. If I was an unusual kid when this started, then I am the oddest dinosaur now—still focused on a concentrated portfolio of individual stocks. But I believe that distraction is a bigger risk than concentration, and too many allocations are *diworsified*.

I like being paid dividends, as a true stakeholder in a business should. I call it mailbox money. One of the best metrics to judge any businesses is: Does it produce increasing cash flow? Anybody can apply the same principle to their own investment plan, which should be treated as a business. Holding a cash dividend payment in your hands is an answer to one of the hardest questions for investors—how do we know what is real or not?

Companies capable of paying and raising dividends from their increasing cash flows dates back hundreds of years for perfectly aligned reasons. It is when either side of that partnership tries to complicate things, that investing gets confusing or worse. Mailbox money I receive as a direct shareholder silences the crowded debates of more growth or income—with a longer-lasting simpler truth. Dividends achieve growth *of* income.

Risk-free reserves

Serving my family, and others who expect to be treated as family, requires that a disciplined plan be built around that stock portfolio. So, while I do not think of it as an investment, I do believe in defense at all times. I have an account full of nothing but insured, tax-free municipal bonds and cash. I do not trade bonds, and I do not forecast interest rates. I do not want to take any risk here.

Peace of mind

A significant influence on how I invest is my business partner, Mike Catalano. He was born and raised in New York, and we had no background in common. We worked together at the largest global bank and brokerage firm. We became the brothers neither of us ever had. There was not one complication, contingency, consultant, or accountant sitting with just the two of us in 2006, at an International House of Pancakes. All we needed was trust, one piece of paper, and great lighting before the crack of dawn. That day we decided to escape Wall Street to launch our own firm. Our "One Page" rule is still applied to all plans.

A good partner can improve anybody's answer to how they invest their own money. Mike's unique experience leads the planning side of our firm, with a transformative impact on peace of mind, mine included. For several years, he kicked tires with actuaries who have the biggest calculators and sharpest pencils for longevity planning. We both hated that longevity was being called a risk by our industry, rather than the ultimate blessing it most certainly is.

After years digging down the defined benefit rabbit holes for company retirement plans, Mike methodically questioned a bias against all annuities. He found only one that he wanted to put our own money in, to build defined benefit personal pensions. I trusted his comprehensive work, and am glad that I did. So, the last account

I invested my own money in was a lifetime income annuity, in my wife's name. That account gives me tremendous peace of mind.

The most important piece of my entire life's puzzle was not planned, but incredible luck—my wife agreeing to marry me. She is not interested in money, never has been. She is fully invested in raising our five kids. I owe her more than saying, "Just trust me." If I have any more good luck, and good health, I am not even at the halftime of life yet. I genuinely hope to never retire. But, if I cannot put our plan on one page for her to clearly understand, no matter what happens, then I have failed. I like knowing she will have zero questions about an insured lifetime income stream.

Underestimated upside

I made one intimidating investment that I knew nothing about. I wanted to own dirt, to sink roots deeper into our operating and belief systems. When we launched an independent firm, a goal was to own our building. As silly and expensive as it appeared, we did not want to pay rent anymore, as our tip of the cap to the Market Gods that we were here to stay for a very long time. My only requirement is that it had to be super close by, so that made it hard. We found a spot that could not have been a bigger mess. We decided to bulldoze through it all and built our company's home from scratch. I knew I would love it, but I underestimated the quality of life investment from a six-minute commute.

My GRINdex account

The only luxury that appeals to me is more choices and grins, with precious time. My favorite allocation is that I coached my kids' sports teams. I get videos made from each season. One was such a miracle that I had to hire a professional from NFL Films because nobody tells a story better (even though I'm a basketball guy). Then, I rented out the nicest movie theater for a party, for the team and community. I stood in the back, hiding with tissues in full blubber after the lights went down.

I would not trade that box of videos for any amount of money in the world. That is not a figure of speech, I mean any actual dollar figure. When hurricanes evacuated my family, twice, it was the only box I took. All the games are great. The conversations in between are better. I call them skull sessions. I love investing that time for my kids, and a lot of other kids outside our neighborhood. No investment will last longer than the memory-making business in others, so I want to make deposits accordingly.

The best trade I ever made was less expectations for more appreciations. I don't know how to properly meditate. I look forward to learning someday. For now, my app-less hack is to slow my heart rate down, close my eyes, and breathe in gratitude and hold it until I tingle. Then, exhale joy.

I enjoy backing that trade by purposefully investing in other people, outside my business and family. I like to donate money to those who need it. But I love to invest in unusual desires to work, which can change more lives for longer. Using the only playbook I know, since my first dollar invested, I believe most in the work part. Sharing money on purpose, to light a curiosity on fire in somebody else who has desire, is my favorite dividend.

How I invest my own money is building around my only stated goal: To never finish.

Lazetta Rainey Braxton

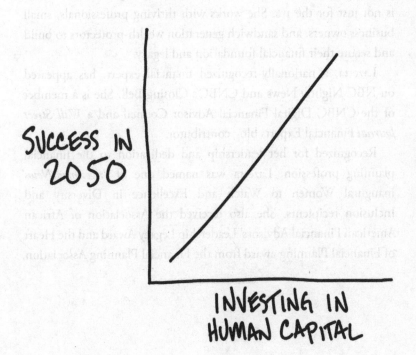

SUCCESS IN
2050

INVESTING IN
HUMAN CAPITAL

Lazetta Rainey Braxton MBA, CFP®, Co-Founder and Co-CEO of 2050 Wealth Partners, is on a mission to provide access to financial planning for "the rest of us." She believes that solid financial advice is not just for the 1%. She works with thriving professionals, small business owners, and sandwich generation wealth-protectors to build and secure their financial foundation and legacy.

Lazetta, a nationally-recognized financial expert, has appeared on NBC Nightly News and CNBC's Closing Bell. She is a member of the CNBC Digital Financial Advisor Council and a *Wall Street Journal* Financial Experts blog contributor.

Recognized for her leadership and dedication to the financial planning profession, Lazetta was named one of *InvestmentNews'* inaugural Women to Watch and Excellence in Diversity and Inclusion recipients. She also received the Association of African American Financial Advisors' Leadership Legacy Award and the Heart of Financial Planning award from the Financial Planning Association.

M Y VERY FIRST investment was in me. In financial terms, the investment or asset is known as human capital. Human capital is when you bring value to an organization by utilizing your skills, knowledge, and experience to advance their financial success. Although I didn't know the term in my earlier years, I understood that being a valuable employee was how you made money. Money was the key to a happy life.

Growing up, money was scarce and financial investments were non-existent. My hardworking, loving parents made it known without hesitation. They earned a living based on their talents as high school graduates. Dad was and remains a construction worker. My mom was a factory worker who later became a Licensed Practical Nurse (LPN) in my adult life. As a high school student, I quickly realized that their income was not enough to support a family of five. They used credit cards to fund shortfalls in income. High interest rates suffocated any chances for them to get ahead financially.

When I turned 16, I landed my first job and added a second one within weeks. I was determined to ease my family's financial burdens. As a naturally-driven person, I excelled in academics, sports, and student-led club activities even while holding two jobs. Building my human capital as a high school student served me well as a prospective college student.

My family's financial situation sparked an obsession in me to learn everything I could about personal finance. My high school didn't offer personal finance courses. Thus, I opted for accounting given my interest in math, business, and money.

My junior year of high school, I discovered a newspaper announcement of a Black female who obtained her license as a Certified Public Accountant (CPA). This historic news in my rural Virginia hometown solidified my interest in pursuing a career in finance. It raised my determination to secure a career that would teach me about finances, pay well, and change the financial trajectory for me and my parents. How I was going to be able to pay for college, however, remained a mystery.

A Division II and Historically Black College and University (HBCU) school offered me a full basketball scholarship. My dad strongly encouraged me to accept given our financial situation. I didn't take his advice, however. I declined the offer and instead decided to attend a Division I school to learn from White, wealthy students. I believed that white, wealthy students could show me the power of and path to money and wealth for use in my community. It was the right decision for me, although my extended family was also disappointed that I didn't celebrate my Black heritage by attending an HBCU. As with high school, I worked two jobs in college to finance my post-secondary education while balancing the demands of rigorous academic work.

My decision to attend the McIntire School of Commerce at the University of Virginia (UVA) paid off. I invested in myself, and built my skills and knowledge during my years as a secondary and post-secondary student, which created the opportunity for me to succeed in corporate America.

A year after graduating from UVA, I met my husband and got engaged. We married the following year. This was my next investment in me and now in us. We both had consumer and student loan debt and pledged that we would pay off the debt as quickly as possible. We also declared our own mantra of having a "Go to Hell" (GTH) fund. We realized early on in our marriage our desire for career flexibility given the employment risks associated with being Black and vocal about diversity and inclusion issues. We also desired to financially support our parents if they needed assistance.

Our plan worked; we paid off over $40,000 in debt in four years by following a debt repayment plan. It wasn't easy, but we followed the plan: We lived off of one income and used the other income to pay off debt and build savings. In addition to being financially prudent, it was also a great foundation for our marriage.

We've tried to be methodical about growing our wealth. Like most beginner investors, we contributed to our employers' retirement plans, starting at a level of the employer match. We also stayed current with tax laws that were investment-related. The year we married, the Taxpayer Relief Act of 1997 passed. It allowed individuals to convert tax-deferred retirement funds to after-tax Roth IRAs and spread the related taxable income from the conversion over two tax years. I took advantage of this opportunity by rolling over a previous employer's plan to a Roth IRA.

The Roth IRA allowed me to select my own investments instead of depending on the investment menu provided by my employer for my 401(k). I chose a socially-conscious and woman-owned fund family, Domini Funds. The financial transaction felt very empowering as an independent, female investor!

In 1998, I accepted an Executive Assistant and portfolio administrator position with an investment management firm and elected to invest in the firm's mutual funds. It was our first joint personal investment. Within two years of marriage, we had a savings account, a debt repayment plan, a taxable investment account, Roth IRAs and 401(k)s.

We advanced to individual 401(k)s—i401(k)—when we both started to earn income from our respective speaking and consulting businesses. When we changed jobs, we consolidated our previous employers' retirement accounts with our tax-deferred i401(k)s. We held onto our Roth IRAs since they cannot be rolled into a Roth i401(k).

Over our 20+ years together, we have used and replenished our GTH fund with the goal of keeping at least six months of expenses. The balance has changed over the years due to our frequent moves, the cost of living based on our residence, and my start-up venture as the owner of a fee-only financial planning firm and Registered Investment Advisor (RIA). Our go-to for cushion savings is money market accounts that are FDIC insured and treasuries when yields are attractive. We also have funds in a Health Savings Account (HSA) which is also a low-yield investment.

Regarding college, taxable and retirement investments, I am a staunch believer in index investing as the core investment and satellite investments to include real estate, stocks, and business ownership. The Thrift Savings Plans (TSP) holds my index fund investments. The TSP, a retirement account for federal employees, has over half a trillion in assets under management and the lowest expense ratio of any financial institution. My husband's primary retirement account is with MMBB, which offers a retirement program for clergy. The clergy-based retirement account grants distributions as housing allowance in retirement. Housing allowance is not subject to ordinary income tax as of today's Internal Revenue Code ruling. Our daughter's 529 plan is held in Vanguard index funds via the New York 529 plan.

Our i401(k)s, IRAs, and our daughter's Coverdell Educational IRA primarily hold stocks of companies that we frequent. We are familiar with their products and services and follow their performance with interest. I have also ventured into stock investments recommended by colleagues in my Roth IRA. I had a couple of holdings that went bankrupt—I took chances on a US-based company and China-based company in two separate industries. Their concept seemed great but their execution didn't live up to its potential and they didn't pivot when trends changed. They served markets that I didn't follow closely. I trusted the *noise*, followed the crowd, and didn't make a move to sell before it was too late. The power of diversification continues to balance out investment gains and losses!

Our real estate portfolio has only one holding—our former primary residence. We rent our Maryland home to continue to build equity at the expense of the renter. The Maryland home will serve as equity for our retirement home, and possibly for another rental property in the future. We are also renters as current New York residents.

Bridging the connection between human capital and financial capital reveals an important observation: My career and that of my husband serve different purposes in our partnership. My husband represents a bond investment—he maintains jobs with steady income and low risk. As an entrepreneur and business owner, I represent an equity investment with higher risk. In 2008, I chose a business model that wasn't commonly adopted—providing financial advice on a fee-for-service basis for middle income clients who didn't believe they could afford the service. To add more risk to the equation, I founded the firm during the start of the housing crisis, and we moved frequently, which resulted in constantly rebuilding my clientele.

Now, trends have changed in my favor. I merged my fee-only financial planning practice with a like-minded female entrepreneur of color. Our firm, 2050 Wealth Partners, is a 100% virtually-based fee-only financial planning firm, operated from our home offices in New York and Maryland. My business partner and I believe in innovation and have our bets on the future promise of being the best stock investment of our lifetimes! We also have the privilege of guiding the human capital and investments of our clients. It's a win-win.

Our founding of 2050 Wealth Partners is our solution to providing guidance to people who are overlooked and underserved by their employers and by Wall Street—people like us, our families, and our communities. Also, we full-heartedly embrace the fact that, by 2050, the US will be an ethnic mosaic. Our desire is to narrow the wealth gap by advancing humanity.

As Gen Xers, my husband and I remain vigilant with pursuing prudent use of human capital and income to support an enjoyable and comfortable life. We desire to live fully into our calling as dedicated spouses, parents of a high school daughter, and professionals who seek to advance the human condition. We are grateful that our values align and that we set the foundation for financial flexibility from the very beginning. It is our prayer that the fruit of our labor will be rewarded during the remainder of our lifetimes and for generations to come.

Marguerita Cheng

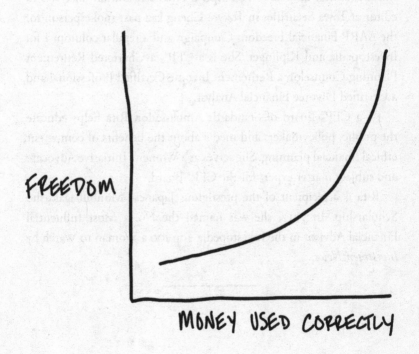

FREEDOM

MONEY USED CORRECTLY

Marguerita M. Cheng is the Chief Executive Officer at Blue Ocean Global Wealth. Prior to co-founding Blue Ocean Global Wealth, she was a financial advisor at Ameriprise Financial and an analyst and editor at Towa Securities in Tokyo. Cheng is a past spokesperson for the AARP Financial Freedom Campaign and a regular columnist for Investopedia and Kiplinger. She is a CFP®, a Chartered Retirement Planning Counselor, a Retirement Income Certified Professional and a Certified Divorce Financial Analyst.

As a CFP® Board of Standards Ambassador, Rita helps educate the public, policymakers and media about the benefits of competent, ethical financial planning. She serves as a Women's Initiative Advocate and subject matter expert for the CFP® Board.

Rita is a recipient of the prestigious Japanese Monbukagakusho Scholarship. In 2017, she was named the No. 3 Most Influential Financial Advisor in the Investopedia Top 100 a Woman to Watch by *InvestmentNews*.

T HE MOST VALUABLE advice that my dad instilled in me was not to define myself by what I have, but rather my accomplishments and education. It is a mantra that I have carried with my family, financial and professional life.

Money should not be the sole determining factor for the decisions made in life. My dad's financial wisdom and insight have enabled me to adopt a balanced, holistic approach to financial matters, for which I am eternally grateful.

My father and his family fled his hometown in Jiangxi province in southern China for Taiwan. He graduated from National Taiwan University in the 1960s with only $17 to his name and the clothes on his back. Even though he was poor in the material and financial sense, he never considered himself poor.

He insisted that while money did not buy happiness, it did provide peace of mind, freedom, and flexibility. I can still hear my dad's voice: "Whatever you do, don't spend money in the dark. Don't squander your money because you're depriving others of precious opportunities and harming those you love."

Discussing financial matters can be stressful for couples. Many people would rather suffer in silence than discuss a personal financial predicament and endure the shame associated with having financial problems or making bad financial decisions.

In American culture, money plays a big part not only in how we see ourselves, but also in how we want others to see us both in our personal and professional lives.

Money means different things to different people based on their experiences and values. My parents would often laugh that they did not fight about money because there was not anything to fight about. When my parents bought their first home, they did not even have enough money to buy a bucket of paint, but they did have an open, honest discussion about their beliefs, thoughts and priorities.

Another nugget of wisdom I learned from my dad is to be open to opportunities as they present themselves and to prepare for tomorrow the best we can.

What I appreciate most about my dad is his ability to engage in discussions about money. When my aunt died unexpectedly with four young kids, my dad paid for her funeral. My uncle asked my dad if he would loan him the money for the funeral. My dad said, "No, I will give you the money. You shouldn't have to worry about this right now."

My dad did not lecture or scold, but he used this as a teaching opportunity about wills and funeral planning.

People may assume that only the rich need to create a will, but the truth is everyone should draw one up. A will outlines your wishes and removes the guesswork after you are gone.

This is wisdom I impart on my clients when talking about uncomfortable topics.

My dad showed me the life insurance policies that he purchased for himself and my mom. He taught me how to crack the safe and how to locate the estate planning documents so that I could take care of mom in case anything happened to him.

He advocated for addressing serious topics on a proactive basis, because if you do not buy life insurance or do not prepare for "what if" scenarios, it does not mean they will not happen.

After graduating with a BA in East Asian Language and Literature, I was awarded a scholarship by the Japanese Ministry of Education to attend Keio University and work in Tokyo, Japan. In my role as an editor/translator of a newsletter for English speaking investors, I applied my communication and analytical skills.

I wanted to apply the concepts I learned in corporate finance, such as healthy balance sheets and strong cash flow statements, to individuals and families so they could protect and grow their net worth while managing their positive cash flow.

My philosophy about money shapes how I invest. I like to build flexibility and discipline in my investment plan. I try to automate my savings and investment plan. I started participating in my 401(k) plan even before I graduated from college.

I have a long-term perspective to investing. I believe that tax diversification is just as important as investment diversification. It is important to have tax-deferred, tax-free and taxable accounts so that you can plan for changes in tax rates. I am not the type of investor who will set it and forget it, nor will I day trade in my account either. Everyone's portfolio deserves TLC.

Financial planning does not mean that you will avert a market downturn, but it does give you certain peace of mind knowing that you can stay the course.

Sometimes, I think people make things more complicated than they need to be. I tend not to become overly optimistic nor overly pessimistic, which my clients really appreciate. I believe in the simple trifecta of dollar cost averaging, tax-free growth and the time value of money.

I recall how excited I was when I learned about 529 plans and opened one up for each one of my children. Because I have taken an entrepreneurial path within the financial advice industry since 2003, I took advantage of the SEP IRA and then the Single K/Individual K/Solo K to help with save money for retirement.

The importance of education is not only how I teach clients but also how I have raised a family. We would not dream of raising illiterate children, so why is financial literacy any different?

Recent studies show Americans have low levels of financial literacy and have difficulty applying financial decision-making skills to real-life situations.

I am an advocate for financial literacy to be taught in schools. What children need is strong communities to help bridge the gap between novice and expert in knowledge of financial literacy.

As a parent, I create an open dialogue with my children. When they ask about finances, I use everyday examples, such as the water or electric bill, to explain the concept of budgeting.

To be honest, the term *financial literacy* can be off-putting. I prefer the terms *financial confidence* and *investor education*. After all, we all could stand to feel more confident about our future.

As the daughter of a Chinese father and American-born mother, I have been exposed to many different stereotypes in the US, Europe, and Asia. I also grew up taking in mixed messages about what it means to be a successful, professional woman.

Indeed, juggling my responsibilities as a daughter, wife, mother, caregiver, professional, and professional financial planner has taught me to strive for balance—not perfection.

When I started out in financial planning, it was rare for a recruited female to be successful with a young family, not to mention one from a diverse background. I knew, and so did everyone else, that the odds were against me. But with my success, over a decade later, that perceived liability is now an asset and a source of inspiration to other young women professionals in the financial planning field.

As young women, they still often hear the message that money is a man's responsibility. That idea paves the way for women not to worry as much about what would happen if they needed to take on multiple caregiver roles and/or be financially independent.

Financial equality and independence are just as important for women. And for those women looking to seek a life of prosperity and build wealth, having the right investing skills is the key. It is very important for women, regardless of their marital status—single, divorced, widowed or married—to take a much more active role in their financial lives.

By taking a more active role, women will gain more clarity, confidence, and control of their lives. To do so, women need to learn as much as possible about money. Like my dad, I instil these values onto my own daughters.

For my clients, I promise them and those they hold dear to their hearts the 4 C's: Clarity, Confidence, Control, and Courage.

Clarity about the options available to them. I want them to focus on what matters to them most. Confidence to plan for their future and know the steps they are taking are right for them. For example, if selecting the lump sum instead of taking the pension keeps them up at night, they need to do what is consistent with their goals and risk tolerance. Control—a sense of what they can control. You can't forecast stock market performance. You can't predict interest rates. You can control how you save, how you spend, how you invest and how you react. Courage—the courage to ask questions and seek help without being judged.

For me, I absolutely love being a CFP® professional because I have the opportunity to transform lives and have a positive impact on my community. Financial planning is intellectually stimulating, emotionally gratifying and financially rewarding.

Alex Chalekian

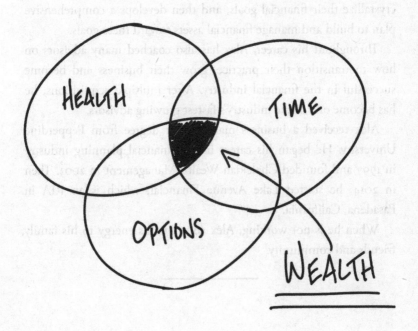

HEALTH

TIME

OPTIONS

WEALTH

Alex Chalekian is the founder and CEO of Lake Avenue Financial. He has been dedicated to assisting his clients in working towards their financial goals for over 20 years. He works diligently to help them crystallize their financial goals, and then develops a comprehensive plan to build and manage financial assets toward these goals.

Throughout his career, Alex has also coached many advisors on how to transition their practice, grow their business and become successful in the financial industry. After multiple acquisitions, he has become one of the industry's fastest growing advisors.

Alex received a business management degree from Pepperdine University. He began his career in the financial planning industry in 1997 and founded Chalekian Wealth Management in 2003. Then in 2014, he started Lake Avenue Financial, which is an RIA in Pasadena, California.

When he is not working, Alex commits his energy to his family, friends and community.

I GREW UP in a house with a lot of love, but not a lot of money. My parents were hard working folks that barely made enough to give me and my brother a decent life.

My mother came to the US in 1970 with her parents—she was a teenager at the time. My dad made his way to this country in 1971 when he was in his late twenties. They met in Los Angeles, got married and decided to raise a family. My brother and I were the first generation in our family to be born in the States.

As kids, we never understood the sacrifices of our parents and grandparents to make sure we were brought up in a safe and healthy environment. They left everything they had in the countries they grew up in and decided to start a new life in the US. After all, this was the land of opportunity, right?

My grandfather, who was the rock in our family, had many skills, but was humble enough to start all over when he came to this country. He, along with my grandmother and mother, worked at any job they could get their hands on. Many times, they would work several shifts in a day, to make sure they could survive. Over the years, my grandfather saved up and eventually opened a small restaurant. This was the first US business started by our family and they were determined to make it a success. My father, who came to the US by himself, also had many skills and was good with his hands. He quickly was offered a job at a jewelry manufacturer in downtown Los Angeles.

After my parents got married, my father kept working in downtown LA and my mom started a job as a teacher. Several years later, they had eventually saved up to buy their first house in Reseda, California. This is the home my brother and I grew up in. It wasn't the fanciest house or the best neighborhood, but my parents were proud to achieve the "American Dream" of being homeowners.

Why am I taking you down memory lane?

Because in order to understand why people invest or want to invest their money in a certain way, I believe that it is especially important to understand people's backgrounds and their first experience of personal finances. It's vital to find out what money means to them and what were their initial experiences that shaped their ideology on wealth.

Wealth means different things to different people. But for me, after watching my family struggle for years, it meant having financial independence. As I have grown older, and hopefully wiser, wealth has taken on a whole different meaning. Wealth now means *health, time* and *options*.

I decided to join the financial industry in 1997 after I realized that I should follow my passion for investing and personal finance. I was 21 at the time and was studying to be an accountant. That's what I thought I wanted to do for the rest of my life.

But while working at an accounting firm as I was attending college, I quickly realized that this wasn't my calling. I recognized that I should set a career path that excited me and motivated me to thrive. At 18, I had already started investing in individual stocks and bought several mutual funds after I graduated from high school. The economics class I took as a senior motivated me to dive into investing.

While I was in college I was able to work, so I would set aside some money and invest it. By 20, I had a small portfolio and was reading *The Wall Street Journal* and *Investor's Business Daily*. A career as a financial advisor seemed like a natural choice for me. After all, I was young and if things didn't work out in the financial industry, I could always try a different career path. But I would still have the knowledge and education that I could use for my own personal benefit.

Early on, I realized that it was important to follow my own recommendations that I was giving to clients. Whether that was setting up a retirement account or investing my clients in the same stocks and mutual funds that I owned. I was not making a lot of money early in my career, so I was eligible to start making small contributions into a Roth IRA. I opted to use growth mutual funds for this account. I realized the importance of diversification and investing in actively managed mutual funds for a $5000 contribution made sense to me.

I also had a taxable brokerage account with several stocks and mutual funds in it. I continued adding money into this account on a monthly basis. Dollar cost averaging might be boring, but it works for investors. I quickly grew this portfolio and honed my skills. Tracking stocks, reading company financials and keeping up with trends was something I did for fun. While most of my friends were trying to figure out what they were going to do with their lives, I was lucky enough to know what I wanted to do with mine.

Fast forward 20 years later, and my current portfolio looks a lot different. Mainly because my largest asset, my financial planning business, has grown over the years. Doing what is best for our clients has helped my firm grow organically, but has also opened up the opportunities for us to acquire other smaller practices. In 2005, I started doing my homework and getting our firm ready for our first acquisition. I quickly realized how the math worked on these transactions and that if the acquisition was done successfully, it would be one of the best investments I would ever make. Knowing this, I set out to find sellers and I closed on my first acquisition in 2008.

Since 2008, I have had several more opportunities to acquire practices, and have closed on those deals if they were the right fit. I quickly realized that cash flow was the key to achieving this financial independence. So, early on in my career, probably in 2000, I specifically focused on financial planning and managing assets for a fee.

As of today, approximately 80% of my assets are in my company stock. As the years have gone by, this number has steadily crept up from 30%. Now, I know that many advisors who are reading this are shaking their heads. We tell our clients to diversify. We tell them to slowly trim their largest stock position to lower their overall risks. We come up with strategies to protect them in the scenario that their company stock drops significantly in value. If I didn't have the opportunity to invest in acquisitions, I would have a larger portfolio of publicly traded stocks and ETFs.

My firm is not a publicly traded company so it doesn't have the liquidity or marketplace that would enable me to sell shares. Instead, this is like one of my small business owner clients that have grown their business to a large portion of their net worth and are waiting for an exit strategy when the time is right. As much as you talk to this client about investing in other things, they have been able to show you how profitable it is for them to reinvest their funds back into the business. And more importantly, they feel like they are in control of their destiny. After all, when you look at the richest entrepreneurs in the world, you will quickly see a pattern: Their largest asset is the business they founded or company stock.

In order to have opportunities to purchase other practices, it was crucial for me to have large cash positions or be cognizant that I might need to liquidate some of my stocks outside of my retirement accounts. The thought process for me was simple: These acquisitions generated great cash flow and a great investment that I could control.

Let's take a look at the following example:

Advisor X generates $100,000 in recurring revenue and has decided to retire.

Advisor X's practice goes on sale for $250,000 (let's use a 2.5 multiple for this example).

I use available cash or some of my investments to purchase the practice for $250,000 and quickly convert it to generate

$100,000 in additional revenue to the firm (financing could also be used for the acquisition).

Assuming I already have the infrastructure in place and don't have any additional expenses from this acquisition, all that revenue should flow down to my bottom line. Based on this example, it would be equivalent to a bond with a 40% coupon. And you would take that cash flow and parlay it into another acquisition. Similar to what many have done with investment properties. The compounding effect over the years can be huge.

Besides the 80% of my assets that are in my business, the remaining 20% are in a mix of cash, individual stocks, ETFs and mutual funds. I don't buy into the argument that you have to choose between active or passive management. Depending on what you are looking to do, you can use either investment option or both.

As of now, I have utilized individual stocks and ETFs for the equity allocation in my portfolios and mutual funds for the fixed income portion. Passive investments like ETFs and index funds are my preference in my retirement accounts. It can help keep the costs low and more importantly stop me from wanting to try and trade in these accounts that are for the long term. In my non-retirement accounts, I prefer holding individual stocks and actively managed funds. Stocks don't always go up, but if I want to take any losses, I want to be able to write them off. I can't do that inside of a retirement account.

As an entrepreneur, you quickly figure out that money is just a means to an end. Being able to take care of and provide for my family is my top priority. As I mentioned before, my definition of wealth means health, time and options. Money is the tool that is needed to help make sure I can keep my family healthy, give them time to do the things they enjoy and the ability to have options in whatever it may be in life.

Take the time to discover what wealth means to you. Once this is crystal clear and you have the blueprint, start laying down the foundation to a happier future.

Conclusion

"Don't tell me what you think, tell me what you have in your portfolio."

—Nassim Nicholas Taleb

T HERE'S AN OLD quip that personal finance is more personal than finance. Though perhaps too clever, this still reveals a truth only sparingly mentioned among serious financial experts: there is no one right way to manage your money.

The orthodoxy—that *right* way—stems from the early days of modern mathematical finance, decades ago. There is received wisdom on optimal portfolios, efficient markets, pricing securities, and other matters in which rational investors can increase their utility.

Below high finance's ethereal plane are the more pedestrian directives on saving smartly, borrowing wisely, and spending prudently. All in, there are rules of the road and we should follow them.

Yet heterodoxy reigns. We know that when elegant theories and simple rules interact with the real lives of individuals and families figuring out how to get by and thrive, managing one's money becomes artful, to say the least.

This book is a collection of short essays from experts in money management who have devoted their careers to the betterment of the financial lives of others. Everyone included knows the orthodoxy.

What should be plain to see is that how practitioners manage their own money is far more an impressionist drawing than a textbook diagram. As Nassim Taleb suggests, you only learn about how someone truly manages money when they show you how they've put their *own* skin in the game. Unlike any other book we know of, these authors have showed you their portfolios.

We gave little direction to the contributors. We shared Josh's original blog and asked them to write their own version. That's about it, other than noting that anything goes, not just on investing *per se*, but saving, borrowing, spending, giving, and so forth.

And what we received back were *stories*. Stories about hope, frustration, joy, struggle, desire, and growth. Human stories. Bob Seawright told the singular tale of a lakeside cottage. Dasarte Yarnway illuminated his family's path from Africa to America. Carolyn McClanahan and Ashby Daniels were among those who shared how trying moments as kids helped forge their ability to thrive as adults.

Money was, and is, an inextricable part of those journeys.

For starters, we must stave off hardship and pay the bills. Across the chapters, we see that the authors have kids to raise, family and communities to support, and causes to underwrite. I'm guessing that nearly every reader of the volume will come across at least one of the essays and say: That's just like me.

In my read of the chapters—and others will have their own takes— several themes jump out.

Money can buy happiness. Yes, I said it. Because it's true. Of course, much pivots on what we mean by "happiness," but the fact is that money solves problems, alleviates pain and regret, and can buy both short-lived thrills and longer-lived joy. Josh Rogers receives joy from his art collection and Shirl Penney from his horses, but both of them and all of the other contributors spoke, in one way or another, about the creation of opportunity that comes with financial flexibility. Ryan Krueger wasn't alone in writing about the "peace of mind" that is possible but not guaranteed when we manage our finances and careers wisely. For those who shared their backstories, I was struck by the sense that they wanted to create something better not just for themselves but, more importantly, for the next generation. The intersection between money and meaning was apparent.

Money is an expression of our values and our identity. I don't believe this point can be expressed strongly enough. Money is a language and we use it to verbalize who we are and who we want to be. When Morgan Housel powerfully articulates the importance of financial independence, he speaks for most people who simply want the option to live the life they desire. For Perth Tolle, the market is one means of expressing her worldview—her business and portfolio are her north star. Josh Brown shared stories of how specific investments are tied to his values and relationships. Many contributors wrote warmly about supporting the causes that matter to them.

Money scripts matter. As Blair duQuesnay illuminates, we are indelibly shaped by our upbringing, which includes the experience of money. The money stories we inherit or those we learn to write ourselves likely weigh more heavily on our decision-making and attitudes than the output of a Monte Carlo simulation. Leighann Miko eloquently described the connection between her upbringing and her current passion for helping others. For both Rita Cheng and Alex Chalekian, family history empowers their advice practices and financial decisions. Debbie Freeman's journey combines both hardship and hope. The shadow of everyone's backstory is cast across their current decisions.

Financial capital is only one of our assets. In a book about money, several contributors wrote about human capital. It makes sense. Each of us has aspirations, with multiple tools to get there. Yes, our wallets matter, but so do our brains and networks. Lazetta Rainey Braxton wrote about investing in herself—her human capital—to forge a good life. So did Dan Egan. Howard Lindzon, Ted Seides, and I leverage our social capital to source better opportunities. This book's first three words—"How I Invest"—open a door to a broader consideration of how we can get ahead.

Process matters and expertise matters. These chapters are practical. We observe detailed techniques for saving, stock picking, portfolio construction, tax management, and retirement planning. Nina O'Neal walked through her strategy for funding her kids' education. Christine Benz has built effective portfolios through her career-long quest for simplicity. Many of the authors spoke to detailed specific retirement strategies. Stories might inspire, but the words and sentences which constitute them are governed by rules. Money, too, has its own grammar and we are best served by learning it. One of the joys in editing this book was seeing firsthand how people I respect built processes for solving problems we all confront.

Investing is a skillful (and personal) art. I grew up in this business evaluating money managers. And what was true decades ago remains true today: there is no one right way to pick stocks and bonds and to build portfolios. Each individual can develop the way that is right for them. Jenny Harrington's dividends and Mike Underhill's commodities are expressions of how they see the world from a vantage point informed by their background and a serious devotion to their craft over many years. They, like others, portray their own path for navigating the world's complexity in a way that works for them.

We are mostly alone in solving common problems—but don't have to be. Financial freedom is hard to achieve without financial literacy, a cause with which many of the contributors, including—and especially—Tyrone Ross, are strongly associated. We recognize that personal discussions of money are uncomfortable among partners, parents, children, and friends. Money is a dangerous topic because it brings an unshakable connection between our bank accounts and our sense of self-worth. Yet in response, our society does a poor job of providing resources and access to those who want to figure it out but don't know where to start.

I know from private conversations with many of the contributors that this exercise was some combination of raw, revealing, and therapeutic. They were given a blank piece of paper and asked: Tell us about *you*—not your clients, not your firm. Despite collectively managing or advising on billions of dollars of other people's money, they proceeded to share personal details in a way they hadn't before. Some expressed anxiety, others shared a sense of relief in telling at least part of their story. *And these are the experts*—people who work with money every day. Thus, it's no surprise that it can be even harder for those who haven't devoted their careers to making sense of the financial world.

So now you have your own blank piece of paper and an opportunity for your own exploration. We hope by sharing these stories, you can better answer the question: How do I invest?

Brian Portnoy
Chicago, 2020

How I Invest…

Write your own essay about how you invest your money here.

_____

_____

_____

_____

_____

_____

_____

_____

_____

_____

_____

_____

_____

_____

_____

_____

_____

_____

_____

_____

_____

_____

_____

_____

_____

_____

_____

_____

_____

_____

_____

_____

_____

_____

_____

_____

_____

_____

_____

_____

_____

_____

_____

_____

_____

_____

_____

_____

_____

_____

_____

_____

_____

_____

CPSIA information can be obtained
at www.ICGtesting.com
Printed in the USA
LVHW040539061220
673468LV00001B/1